MW01596462

# Righteousness By Faith

*Transcription*
*of*
Larry
Wilson

THE LADDER OF FAITH IS EVER ONWARD AND UPWARD

# RIGHTEOUSNESS BY FAITH

First edition, October 2021 | All rights reserved.
Copyright © 2021
ISBN 978-0-9848102-1-5

Scriptural quotations taken from The Holy Bible, New International Version® NIV® Copyright© 1973 1978 1984 2011 by Biblica, Inc.™

Used by permission. All rights reserved worldwide.

Larry W. Wilson

Wake Up America Seminars, Inc.
P.O. Box 273, Bellbrook, Ohio 45305
(800) 475-0876

*On occasion, italics and brackets in Scripture quotations have been added to enhance understanding. They are not intended to change the meaning of the texts, only to clarify. We encourage you to consider them and hope they will provide you with deeper insight as you study God's Word.*

Illustrations by Polina Hrytskova

BOOKS BY
## Larry W. Wilson

The Untold Story of Jesus (2019)

No More Delay (2018)

The Lamb's Book of Life (2016)

Jesus' Final Victory (2011)

Daniel Unlocked For the Final Generation (2003)

Bible Stories with End Time Parallels (2002)

Warning! Revelation is About to be Fulfilled (1989)

# Acknowledgments

This book could never have been created by one person alone. In addition to what I myself was able to do, special appreciation is due to Marty, Diana, Shelley, Eunice, and Heidi. We are also deeply indebted to all who generously support this ministry.

Rex Johnson

# Table of Contents

DEDICATED TO THE MEMORY OF
LARRY W. WILSON

# Foreword

To say that I am thrilled to write the foreword for Larry Wilson's book *Righteousness by Faith* is an understatement! The *Righteousness by Faith* seminar in 1998, in my opinion, is the most powerful series Larry ever did. Not only is *Righteousness by Faith* the greatest story in the Bible, it is also the most incredible love story you'll ever read. The way Larry presents the subject is undoubtedly Holy Spirit enabled, for there is simply no other explanation for how well it was done.

It changed my life forever.

When I started the manuscript, my original plan was to simply transcribe Larry's video series. I enjoy listening to audio or watching video but learn best when reading. Therefore, because I wanted to understand *Righteousness by Faith* well enough to share with others, I needed it in print. As several years passed, however, I thought *Why not make this into a proper book?* Well, let me tell you, converting a week-long seminar from audio into a book, while retaining the author's voice and style, is difficult and time consuming.

It has taken many years (literally) to turn the *Righteousness by Faith* video series into a readable format. In fact, I was working on transcribing it when the twin towers were hit in 2001. Who but the Lord could have known that Larry and Marty would ask me to work with Wake Up 18 years later, providing the opportunity to publish *Righteousness by Faith*.

It's my hope that Larry would be pleased with this book, and that the Lord will be greatly honored through it.

Rex Johnson

*"Keep your mind and heart open to the Holy Spirit...you will be hearing from Him."*

— *Larry Wilson*

# Editor's Note

You will notice this book reads and feels differently than previous books published by WUAS. There are two reasons for this.

1) In the past when Larry sent manuscripts to the office, the office would pore through his writings and make grammatical and other edits to make for a "better, more professional" book.

Most of the time, because he had already spent much effort writing and rewriting his manuscript as many as five times, Larry would often concede to the changes so he could tackle the next project. His hope was that the spirit and idea of what he originally wrote would come through and influence people's lives to God's glory. He would, however, occasionally voice frustration that the final product had lost his voice and didn't sound like him.

If you've ever received a long email from Larry, you'll know that he wrote how he spoke. To read something Larry wrote was like having a one-on-one conversation with him. He knew his audience and wrote directly to them. Larry was a clear thinker, and his writing style was clear and clutter free; it was natural, comfortable, and warm. That's how writing should be. Unless of course, one is writing a scientific treatise or a technical manual for repairing carburetors, and who wants to read that?

2) Larry didn't actually write the manuscript for this book. He spoke it. It is derived from a transcription of Larry's 1998 Durango seminar titled *Righteousness by Faith*. When I first talked with Larry about putting this book together, he said with a grin on his face, "I not only give you my blessing, but I'll also pray for you."

Before his death in January 2021, he graciously shared many emails, suggestions, and answered many questions to help make this book a reality. His only request was that it "sound" like him. Larry felt good writing should be heard, not seen; comfortable and unstilted, not stiff and mechanical; and so we've gone to great lengths to make sure his voice (the words he used) and writing style (authenticity) remain intact for the most part.

As you read, you may notice a few "formal writing" faux pas we allowed to go to press. We humbly ask you to overlook them and simply enjoy Larry Wilson in (mostly) his own words.

I really miss him.

Rex Johnson

# Introduction

In this book, specific biblical topics integrate harmoniously to create a beautiful story—a compelling story that has no equal. I have found nothing else like it on Earth. And, after you understand it, you will never be the same!

I sincerely encourage you to read each page with an open heart and mind, allowing the Holy Spirit to reveal something of value. But before you begin chapter one, I want to tell you a few things so as you progress, you'll have some perspective in which to put the concepts you find.

First, this book is not endorsed, sponsored, affiliated, nor associated with any religious group, church, or organization. I say this up front because many religious people will only read materials that are published by their church, and as far as I know there aren't any churches that teach what I have written. Although this book contains many concepts you have probably never heard, it wasn't written to convert the world to my views or understanding of truth. I simply offer it as a student of God's Word, sharing the marvelous things I've learned of His love and the wonderful plans He has for His people.

Second, I believe salvation comes through faith in Jesus Christ, not denominational affiliation. I hope this book's message will help you develop a more clear understanding of this good news, and that you will consider the concepts offered and be encouraged to share them with your family, friends, and neighbors. My goal is to educate, stimulate, and inspire readers with a more complete understanding of God *and His Word* because ultimately nothing else matters.

Third, the conclusions and doctrines presented are based

on the Bible and the Bible alone. I believe the Bible is the only book in the world that reveals the truth about God, and I accept no other authority when it comes to faith or spiritual matters. I do this confidently because I've proven the validity of the Bible to myself after several years of skepticism. You may be at the same skeptical place in your life. If so, read on!

Fourth, there are five essential truths that every Christian should know, and the summery of these five truths is called the *gospel*. Think of these five as being closely related siblings. The subject of this book, *righteousness by faith*, is the first truth of the five.

1) *Salvation by faith*
2) *Sabbath*
3) *State of man in death*
4) *Sanctuary*
5) *Second coming of Jesus*

Last, I am not a prophet or an authority, nor do I claim to know it all. Therefore, I don't ask you to believe what I believe, only that you consider things you may not presently understand. I offer this statement because any time two people talk about religious issues, one believes something the other doesn't. This is why there are over 9,000 Christian denominations in the world. Christians have a hard time seeing things the same way, and they aren't alone. Muslims and Jews, too, have many different sects. All religious systems are fragmented in a number of ways. So, as you read, please be patient. It takes a while to define and integrate multiple concepts into one harmonious whole, and I can't do it in 20 pages—it's just too big.

I believe we are on the verge of the spectacular events that will inaugurate the end of the world and Christ's coming. In fact, I am looking forward to it because I'm anticipating going home!

Those words "going home" remind me of a valuable lesson learned the day after returning home from the Vietnam War. It is the experience that made me consider the cost of *righteousness by faith* for the very first time. It's the experience that made me appreciate what only Christ could do for me.

When I left the jungle, it was about 114 degrees. When I arrived at Fort Dix, it was minus 4. Jungle fatigues were made out of nylon, a very thin material, and when we landed there was about 6 inches of snow on the ground. But the cold didn't matter. I was so glad to have made it back to the states, I ran out and got down on my hands and knees and kissed the ground.

The Army issued us some clothing in exchange for our jungle wear so we could fly home. I got home about 10:30 p.m., and mom was still at work—she was working as an LPN at the hospital. Mom came home about an hour later and the joy of reunion was inexpressible. What a wonderful evening. I was home again! The memory is so emotional for me even after 45 years.

The next morning I got up and mom looked at me and said, "Well son, you have no clothes to wear. We threw everything away when you left."

I said, "You WERE expecting me to return, weren't you?"

"Yes, of course," she replied. "But we didn't think you would want clothes you had outgrown."

Without saying a word, she went to her purse and took out her paycheck—she had been paid the night before—endorsed it, and laid it on the table. Knowing how hard and how difficult her work was, and to see that 80 hours of work lying on the table, I couldn't take that check.

That was my first encounter with understanding my need for the righteousness of Christ. What He paid to give me the clothing I needed to receive salvation. How do you measure that?

Now, I want to get into the most important and thrilling part of the *plan of salvation*, and try to explain the details of *righteousness by faith* so that you can see the whole beautiful story of how God is going to save mankind.

*"I don't ask you to believe what I believe, only that you consider things you may not presently understand."*

# CHAPTER 1

─────

# Why Faith is Crucial

The topic and title of this book is one of the most profound subjects in all the Bible, *Righteousness by Faith*. A different title could read, *What Must I Do to Be Saved?* An even shorter title could be, *Jesus Saves*. The story on the following pages should be of great encouragement. And it's my hope that when you finish the book, you'll have a deeper sense of God's great love and His mercies upon His children.

This study was written in the context of four books of the Bible for the same reason the four gospels were written by four different men. Do you know why the Lord had the gospels written by Matthew, Mark, Luke, and John? Because no one person can see it all; no one person can accurately understand truth as it is in Christ. So by having four different people write the story of Christ's life and ministry and work on Earth, we learn by putting pieces together, things we would not otherwise know. For example, Matthew is a converted Jew. And in Matthew 24:15–16 he quotes Jesus as saying, **"So when you see standing in the holy place 'the abomination that causes** desolation,' spoken of through the prophet Daniel [and then parenthetically it says]—**let the reader understand**—[as though we could] **then let those who are in Judea flee to the mountains.**"

And then Luke, the converted Gentile, in Luke 21:20–21 quoting Jesus writes the same verse but says it entirely differently.

He says, "**When you see Jerusalem being surrounded by armies, you will know that its desolation is near. Then let those who are in Judea flee to the mountains.**"

The contrast between these two verses demonstrates that the ear of the Jew, Matthew, and the ear of the Gentile, Luke, heard the same sermon and came away with a little different understanding; because the abomination that causes desolation is a Jewish expression, not a Gentile expression. And so we need Luke to help us understand Matthew, and we need Matthew to help us understand Luke.

This is why, to give the subject balance, I have chosen four books of the Bible to demonstrate and explain *righteousness by faith*. I believe Romans defines what *righteousness by faith* is, James shows how it's applied, Hebrews exalts it, and Revelation demonstrates its ultimate triumph.

### The Beginning

There is so much confusion in our world today, and I think a lot of it has to do with where people start in understanding God's Word. If we're going to understand certain issues and developments and problems that are interpretive in Scripture, we have to start at their beginning to understand them. Righteousness by faith is no different. We must go back to its beginning if we are to understand why it's so important.

Notice what God told Adam in the garden right after He created him. He said, "**But you must not eat from the tree of the knowledge of good and evil, for when you eat from it you will certainly die.**"

In the King James Version it's translated even more emphatically: it reads, **"For in the day that thou eatest thereof thou shalt surely die."**[1]

This is the first covenant *before* sin on Earth.

I understand from the verse that if Adam and Eve should ever eat of the fruit of this tree, they were to be executed *that very day* because the wages of sin is death by execution. Execution is the emphasis.

Today, we use the electric chair or lethal injection for capital punishment. In Jesus day, it was the cross. Jesus was executed. He did not die of old age. In the sanctuary service, no lamb died of old age; and neither will the wicked at the end of the 1,000 years.

What happens to the wicked at the end the millennium? The Bible says, "Fire from God comes down from heaven and burns them up!"[2]

The wages of sin is not withering away. That's the consequence of sin, not the penalty for sin. You must understand, there is a difference between the consequence of sin and the penalty for it. Let me illustrate by using common insurance language.

### Consequence vs Penalty

Let's say you're driving your car too fast and fall off the shoulder of the road, hit a tree, and injure yourself terribly.

What happens when the policeman arrives and assesses the scene, measures the skid marks, and discovers you were doing 105 mph and lost control of your car?

Before the officer is through with you, you will have a clear understanding of both penalty and consequence. Penalty (ticket) for having broken the law by exceeding the speed limit, and consequence (pain) as a result of the injury you're suffering from.

---

[1] Genesis 2:17. (Direct quotes from the Bible are in double quotes *and* bolded.)

[2] Revelation 20:9. (Larry's paraphrase of Bible text are in double quotes but *not* bolded.)

There are two separate effects from wrongdoing. Now, they may not be recognized at the same time but, inevitably, both are always exacted.

In the beginning, when God created Adam and Eve, He gave them a very clear understanding of what would happen on the day they ate of this tree. In Genesis 2:17, He said, **"For when you eat from it you will certainly die."**

### Eve Deceived

I can almost hear the muffled conversation and sophistry used when Lucifer called to Eve as she was wandering by the tree, "Psst... Eve... Hey Eve."

When she turned toward him he asked her, "Has God said you cannot eat of this tree?"

"Yes," she replied, "God said we can't touch it or we'll die." She misquoted God and was trapped by her own misunderstanding. God didn't say they couldn't 'touch it,' he had only said they couldn't 'eat it.' Yet, here was this wonderfully beautiful snake eating this fruit.

The snake said to her, "Ah, Eve, this is so good!"

Now, the Bible doesn't say the snake was eating the fruit. It only says, **"When the woman SAW that the fruit of the tree was good for food."**[1] I think the devil demonstrated that to her. The Bible doesn't use those words but it's what I understand from the story.

And the curious thing was that when Eve ate the fruit she didn't immediately die. The Bible says, **"She also gave some to her husband, who was with her, and he ate it."** And then they ran for cover.

### Adam Succumbs

I believe one of the reasons Adam succumbed to temptation was because Eve didn't immediately die. The Bible doesn't say that, I'm simply suggesting it. Adam was probably scratching

---

[1] Genesis 3:6

his head in wonderment when he saw Eve handling the fruit. What Adam did not know (and could not have known) was, on that day, as the executing angel was leaving heaven to come and destroy the guilty pair, Jesus stepped in the way and, at that very moment, became man's intercessor! This is why Jesus is called an intercessor. He stood in the way and deferred the justice that was to be executed upon the guilty pair.

I can imagine Jesus running to the Father and saying, "Let ME take their place. Let ME die in their place. Let ME die for them." And ever since that day, the justice that God's law requires has been delayed. But that justice is coming, because at the end of the story the wicked will be destroyed. Their execution will be implemented, and then the justice and law of God will be put right.

In Genesis 3:8-9, Adam and Eve ran and hid in the bushes; and then in the evening, the Bible says, "In the cool of the day, Jesus, the creator of Adam and Eve, the maker himself came calling, 'Adam, Eve, where are you?'" He knew where they were, but He still came calling.

This is the story throughout God's Word. The whole of the gospel is about God calling us, not us calling God. It is about God seeking man, not man seeking God. He came to their home calling, "Adam, Eve, where are you?" He could just as easily be calling your name and asking, "Where are you?"

When man was created, he was righteous in every way. He had done no wrong. He was perfect. When God had finished creating man He said, "Oh, this is good!" Well, after they ate the fruit, the Lord called the snake, the man, and the woman together and had a little conference. And God begins the meeting by addressing the snake, **"Because you have done this, cursed are you above all livestock and all wild animals! You will crawl on your belly and you will eat dust all the days of your life."**[1]

A number of Bible scholars surmise that at this time snakes

---
[1] Genesis 3:14

probably flew and were very beautiful creatures. The Bible says, "the serpent was the most subtle creature of all of God's creation, and that which became cursed is now the most ugly and feared of all creatures."[1] This was the curse that came upon the serpent.

### Function of Covenants

I mentioned earlier the first covenant *before* sin. Genesis 3:15 brings out the first covenant *after* sin. So before going further, let me explain how covenants work. A covenant is like a law that is perpetual and applicable to all who come under its dominion.

If you own a piece of real estate and you decide to divide it into smaller pieces and sell off some of the parcels, as the owner of the land, it is within your right and privilege to set up covenants that go with the land; and whoever buys the land, from then onward, submits to that covenant.

The idea is that covenants are perpetual and ongoing. And if in the covenant you say, "I want no junk cars on this property," that specification goes with the land.

Now don't get hung up on this. I know covenants can be amended. But I'm using this to illustrate the point that covenants, when created, are intended to be perpetual.

When God told Adam and Eve in Genesis 2:17, **"You must not eat from the tree of the knowledge of good and evil, for when you eat from it you will certainly die,"** that was a covenant.

The reason God is so strong in His language, and acknowledges that He would kill them for disobedience, is illustrated in Drawing 1.1. The illustration explains how God created Adam and Eve and why the wages of sin is death.

### Magnetic Poles

Notice that Adam has a big magnet around him, and this

---

[1] 2 Corinthians 11:3

*Drawing 1.1*

magnet has a positive pole and a negative pole. Suppose that the positive pole represents righteousness (doing right), and the negative pole represents rebellion (doing wrong).

When Adam was created initially he was attracted, by his very nature, to do what was right. He had, built-in, the propensity for right doing.

God created Adam and Eve with the same kind of nature that He has. For them to intentionally do wrong required a great act of the will; it was not easy, it was not ordinary, it was not common, it was not something they would naturally do.

Doing what was right and holy was their natural disposition. This is how God created them.

But when they sinned, the magnetic poles changed. Instead of being attracted to right doing, Adam and Eve took on a fallen nature and became attracted to wrongdoing.

Because of this, the offspring of Adam and Eve, all of us, have been cursed with a propensity for wrongdoing (by our nature) ever since that day. To emphasize this, remember that the firstborn of Adam and Eve turned out to be a murderer. Cain killed his brother Abel. One generation removed from the garden produced a manslayer.

The reason that the wages of sin is death by execution is that God will not allow His universe to become filled with individuals having a natural disposition for doing evil. For in no time at all, these created beings would take the place of God, usurp the authority of God, destroy God, and become God if they could.

You know the story of Lucifer and why he's the way he is. Lucifer is what happens when the original nature is changed.

This is why Jesus said to Nicodemus, "Except a man be born again he cannot get into heaven."

And what does being born again mean?

It means that you add another nature, a nature like Adam and Eve had in the beginning; one that is attracted to right doing, one that begins to love the ways of God because of what the Spirit is doing within you, a nature with which you begin to love holiness.

Yes, the old carnal nature is still there. Yes, you still have the old self inside. But that nature isn't in charge—it's not in control.

Paul had been a Christian nearly 35 years when he wrote Romans 7:19. In there he says, **"For I do not do the good I want to do, but the evil I do not want to do—this I keep on doing."**

Why does he say this?

Because he recognized that in the flesh there is distress. He had in his flesh the carnal body but in his mind the Spirit of God, and the two were always fighting each other.

The great reformer, Martin Luther, when he was investigating righteousness by faith, came to the conclusion that, even with the warring of our two natures, sin remains. But when a person is born again sin doesn't reign, because sin is no longer on the throne of the human heart—Jesus is.

Adam and Eve lost more than their garden home when they sinned; they also lost access to the tree of life. Even more importantly than those two things, they lost a nature having a propensity to do right

When you raise little children, do you teach them to do wrong or right? Parents know you have to train children to do right because it's their natural disposition to do wrong. And I'm talking about toddlers who know nothing about realities. It's just their nature; that's the big problem.

In Genesis 3:15 the Lord is speaking to the serpent and says, **"I will put enmity between you** [mister snake] **and the woman."** Enmity means mutual hatred. God is saying, "I will put animosity between the two of you." The snake and the woman are going to be at odds with each other. The verse continues, **"And between your offspring and hers."** The snake and the woman will both have offspring.

I wrote earlier that covenants are given because they are perpetual in nature. They're meant to be everlasting. Now, there are different kinds of covenants. Some types are made unilaterally.

A unilateral covenant is when a declaration is made and no matter what the parties involved say, it cannot be changed. This type of covenant can only be decreed by one having the power and authority to enforce it.

Genesis 3:15 is an example of a unilateral covenant. No matter what Adam, Eve, and the snake may have said, argued about, or agreed upon, it had nothing to do with what God said He was going to do. His statement is one-sided. God declared it, decreed it, and that's the way it's going to be. There is no voting, no negotiating, no arguing. This by definition is unilateral.

God said, **"I will put enmity between you and the woman,**

and between your offspring and hers." And we also read in
Revelation 12:17, **"Then the dragon was enraged at the woman and went off to wage war against the rest of her offspring."**
We start with the woman in Genesis and end with the woman
in Revelation. The woman represents the people of God, and
the serpent represents the people of the devil.

How can there be people of the devil?

Simple. Jesus said, "Unless a man is born again he really is
of the devil." What this means is, "Unless you are born again
you really are the offspring of your father, the devil."

*The Snake*

Let's go back to Genesis 3:15. Notice that all of a sudden
the word "he" is injected into the verse. This is referring to
someone of the offspring of the woman, **"He will crush your
head** [mister serpent]."

It is the first inkling that an intercessor would be coming to
bring redemption. This is a tiny clue that meant a great deal to
Adam and Eve.

Now that we live nearly 6,000 years later and we know a
whole lot more about the story, it isn't of such profound interest to us as when the Lord said it directly to them.

Jesus is speaking to Lucifer.

Remember, these two former close friends had already had
a fight in heaven.

Jesus is saying to the serpent, "I will put hatred between you
and the woman, between your offspring and hers, and he will
crush your head."

The best way to kill a snake is to crush its head. I have never
seen anyone beat on the tail of a snake to kill it.

And then Jesus, with a sense of foreknowing sorrow, says,
**"And you** [Lucifer] **will strike his heel** [but it won't be fatal]."

It's interesting that Lucifer—the fallen angel who was clos-
est and best of friends with Christ in heaven—kills Jesus, but

then, in the end, Jesus destroys Lucifer. What a tragic story of two close friends.

*Obligation of Law*

When God put Adam and Eve in the Garden of Eden, He put them under the obligation of law. Notice the word LAW in Drawing 1.1.

What was the law in the garden? Not to eat of the tree. And what was the penalty for breaking the law? Death by execution.

How quickly was the penalty to be carried out? **"In the day that thou eatest thereof."**

That sounds like a terrible thing to say to creatures you love, but there is good reason for it to be this way.

Go to Genesis 3:21. This verse takes place one evening in the garden. Speaking of Jesus, the Bible says, **"The Lord God made garments of skin for Adam and his wife and clothed them."** What is God doing? What does this mean?

That evening in the garden, the guilty naked pair—fully exposed for their wrongdoing, their shame showing everywhere—stand still before Jesus. Jesus then takes a lamb and kills it, and with its hide makes garments to clothe His children so that their nakedness and shame are not exposed.

This is a beautifully symbolic story of Christ covering the guilty pair with His own righteousness. Everything God is doing in the story is to teach and explain how salvation works, how it comes about, and what it costs.

I wonder—as Adam and Eve stood there looking at the lamb's carcass, feeling the garments against their skin—what was running through their minds. Remember, they were very intelligent creatures fresh from God's hand.

And as they thought about the covering of God's righteousness, as they looked at the price for this covering, I'm sure they had a sorrow and agony that you and I cannot comprehend.

The point I want to make, and hope you take away, is that

God Himself provided the clothing. The good news is that God Himself provides the righteousness we need to be saved. And the message of this book is how to acquire that righteousness.

Notice what Genesis 3:22 brings out. This is the Son talking to the Father. **"And the Lord God said, 'The man has now become like one of us, knowing good and evil.'"** What does He mean by "knowing good and evil"?

Prior to Lucifer sinning, none of the creatures of heaven had any knowledge of evil; they had never seen it, they had no example of it, they had nothing to measure or understand it by. There was no way for them to comprehend evil.

When Jesus created Adam and Eve, I'm certain He told them about Lucifer and to be wary of any tricks that might come, but they really had no knowledge of evil. The knowledge of evil was only in the mind of God; and that's why the Bible says of man, **"So the Lord God banished him from the Garden of Eden to work the ground from which he had been taken. After he drove the man out, he placed on the east side of the Garden of Eden cherubim and a flaming sword flashing back and forth to guard the way to the tree of life."**[1]

Now, the next section is something you will have to really think about because it's critical that you understand.

### Two Types of Death

When Adam and Eve were expelled from the garden, the penalty of death by execution was delayed because of the presence of an intercessor. This delay brought about another turn of circumstances which produces sleep. What do I mean by 'sleep'? I mean death.

Refer back to Drawing 1.1. Adam lived to be 930 years of age. We don't know how long Eve lived.

(Incidentally, the Bible doesn't indicate the cause of death for either of them, but they probably died of laryngitis. If you have children you will understand why!)

---

[1] Genesis 3:23

All people lived to be of a great age prior to the flood, probably because of the properties of the tree of life. Adam and Eve had *conditional* immortality, and as long as they could get to the tree of life they could live and enjoy life forever.

When God banished them from the garden and prevented their access to the tree, it was so that they would eventually wear out and go to sleep. Fifty-three times in the New Testament, death is referred to as sleep.

In the story of Lazarus, when Lazarus had died, the Lord said, "**I am going there to wake him up.**" And the disciples replied, "**Lord, if he sleeps, he will get better.**"[1] Then Jesus explained, "I'm not talking about the sleep you have every night, I'm talking about going to sleep in death, awaiting the resurrection."

The reason the Bible calls death 'sleep' is because it is temporary. For us here on Earth, God has set our years to be about threescore and ten. Some do a little better, some do a little worse. So we have two types of death:

*1) Eternal Destruction – death by execution, which is permanent.*
*2) Sleep – the consequence of sin, which is temporary.*

Now, when God created Adam and Eve, He put them under the obligation of law. And the penalty for breaking God's law is death by execution. Look at Drawing 1.2.

When Jesus stepped in the way and became man's Intercessor, we call this grace or mercy. Think of grace as an escape plan from the penalty of death by execution. Undeserved grace was placed between the guilty pair and the execution they were to receive.

I need to explain something which is a little difficult to grasp at first. When God created Adam and Eve, they had the ability to have offspring. From the start, God told them to be fruitful and multiply—but there were no children born in the garden. Adam and Eve were neither fruitful nor did they multiply

---

[1] John 11:11–12

*Drawing 1.2*

before they sinned. It's my calculation (best guess) that they lived in the Garden of Eden about a 40 years prior to sinning. Well, after they sinned and began to have offspring, the nature of their two boys, Cain and Abel, were very different.

### Two Natures

In Genesis 4:1–3 the Bible says, **"Adam made love to his wife Eve, and she became pregnant and gave birth to Cain. She said, 'With the help of the Lord I have brought forth a man.'"** She was thrilled, little baby Cain! **"Later she gave birth to his brother Abel. Now Abel kept flocks, and Cain worked the soil."**

Notice that Cain was a farmer and Abel was a herdsman. Farmers and herdsmen do not like each other. There is a perpetual contest between the two. They are antagonistic by nature. The two use land and see its resources entirely differently. **"In the course of time Cain brought some of the fruits** of the soil as an offering to the Lord."

Now understand, the Bible doesn't always tell us everything we need to know outright. But if we study Scripture closely, everything we need to know will be found.

Follow the scenario. **"In the course of time Cain brought some of the fruits of the soil as an offering to the Lord."**

Do you think Cain just arbitrarily decided to bring some fruit and create an altar and present it to the Lord, or do you suppose that there was an obligation that God required sacrifices at prescribed times, even at this early time?

Up to this point, the Bible hasn't said anything about sacrifices being proscribed.

But notice Genesis 4:4–5. **"And Abel also brought an offering—fat portions from some of the firstborn of his flock."**

How would Abel know to bring fat from the firstborn? His father had told him the story, and what was required of Adam and Eve was required of their descendants. That's how covenants work. Abel brought what was required.

The Bible continues, **"The Lord looked with favor on Abel and his offering, but on Cain and his offering he did not look with favor. So Cain was very angry, and his face was downcast."** Interpreted this means, "bottom lip extended."

The Lord asked Cain, **"Why are you angry? Why is your face downcast?"** He's asking, "Why are you so upset?" Then the Lord said, **"If you do what is right."**[1]

This is a clue. Cain knew what was right because God had expressed what was right. God had told those two young men what to do, but Cain would not and did not do it.

Conversely, the Bible says, Abel DID what was right. But understand, although Abel did what God required, his works did not produce righteousness; his faith produced the righteousness.

Let me explain the process so that when we begin to put all

[1] Genesis 4:7

*Drawing 1.3*

of the pieces together, we can build a solid understanding of how precious the gift of God's righteousness really is. 1 John 3:12 says, **"Do not be like Cain, who belonged to the evil one and murdered his brother."**

In the covenant of Genesis 3:15, the Lord clearly identifies both the offspring of the snake and the offspring of the woman. Notice who John says Cain is the offspring of—the snake—the serpent! **"And why did he murder him? Because his own actions were evil and his brother's [actions] were righteous."** I need to explain what is taking place because, at first, it's a little hard to understand.

### Two kinds of Righteousness

Look at Drawing 1.3. The first thing to realize is there are two kinds of righteousness. One is the righteousness that comes from God. It is produced by God, made by God, belongs to God. This kind of righteousness has nothing to do with man. JESUS represents this kind of righteousness.

Next, there is another kind of righteousness that Paul speaks of as holiness. Holiness is when we reorder our lives in conformity to the will of God: Thou shalt not kill or steal or commit adultery or take the name of the Lord in vain, etc.

When we keep and observe God's laws, we are establishing a kind of human holiness. LARRY represents this kind of righteousness. But this type is not to be confused with the righteousness of God.

In Romans 1:17, notice what the Bible says. **"For in the gospel the righteousness of God is revealed—a righteousness that is by faith from first to last, just as it is written: 'The righteous will live by faith.'"** Paul says that in the gospel a righteousness from God is revealed.

Now jump to Romans 3:21–22 and notice what he says there. **"But now apart from the law the righteousness of God has been made known, to which the Law and the Prophets testify. This righteousness is given through faith in Jesus Christ to all who believe. There is no difference between Jew and Gentile."**

Paul is saying that there is a righteousness from God apart from observing the law. He is talking about a righteousness from God that has nothing to do with the holiness that comes from conformity to God's law.

These two verses are describing two separate and distinct kinds of righteousness. You must understand this profound point for the topic to make sense.

There are two kinds of righteousness. One comes by faith APART FROM DOING what God requires. The other comes by DOING what God requires—obeying His laws.

Maybe this simple illustration will help.

If you drive 55 miles per hour and the speed limit is 55 miles per hour, the law declares you to be righteous. I have just described the righteousness that comes from right doing—obeying the law.

Let me give another illustration of these two forms of righteousness. Look at Drawing 1.3 again. Notice the Ten Commandments which represents the law.

In the beginning, there was law. God has always had law; therefore, all of His creatures are under the obligation of law. Adam and Eve were under the obligation of law even in their saved condition while in the Garden of Eden. They understood, "Do not eat of the tree of the knowledge of good and evil."

Lucifer and his angels were under the obligation of law before they fell; and the reason they fell is because they refused to comply. This is called rebellion.

*Angels Are Recording*

Notice the large book that has been opened in Drawing 1.3. When Jesus was born, an angel began documenting (recording) the life of Christ. Jesus lived on Earth about 33 years, and the little black lines in the illustration represent the entries in heaven's journal of Jesus' sinless life.

The Bible says that in Christ there was no sin. This means the law looked at Jesus and declared Him to be Righteous. There has never been any fault in Him.

When I was born, my recording angel began documenting my life. You can see my life (Larry) on the right-hand side. The black lines represent 70+ years of recording, and the little red squiggly lines represent sin. Know that every page of our lives has something on it.

When the law looks at me, it declares me to be guilty because I'm a sinner. The Bible says, "For all have sinned and come short of the righteousness that the law requires."[1]

One day, the Holy Spirit (represented by the dove) came to me and spoke to my heart and said, "Larry I'd like for you to consider the verdict. You have been condemned to death and will be executed in due time. The wages of sin is death and you are facing execution."

---

[1] Romans 3:23

And then He said, "The good news is, you don't have to die. The Lamb of God has died in your place if you are willing to accept Him as Lord and Master of your life. If you are willing to live by faith, the Lord will give you His righteousness."

What this meant in practical terms was, God was calling me to live by faith. To go where He said go, be all that He required me to be, and do all that He wanted of me.

He then said, "If you will do this—if you will live by faith— the most wonderful thing will happen. God will take the scissors of His righteousness, cut the life of Christ out of the book, and lay that life over yours (red perforated lines in drawing). This means that when the Father looks at you, He will see you as though you never sinned!"

This is called justification by faith. Justification means: just as though you have never sinned."

I think it was the evangelist George Vandeman who said, "When I look at myself, I don't see how I can be saved. But when I look at what Jesus is offering, I don't see how I can be lost."

I am describing the righteousness that comes from God! Jesus is God. He is our Creator, our Maker, our Friend, our High Priest, our Intercessor—He's everything! And He offers His righteousness for free, if we are willing to live by faith!

Now understand, going and being and doing does not change the fact that I'm a sinner; once a sinner, always a sinner.

1 John 1:8 says, **"If we claim to be without sin, we deceive ourselves and the truth is not in us."** This means in plain English that we are lying—and that's a sin.

I had a man once tell me that he had not sinned in the last twenty-two years. I said, "Well sir, your standard of righteousness is very low."

Now, technically, he didn't claim to have never sinned. But if one can believe that he hasn't sinned in twenty-two years, he is deceiving himself as the verse states.

The book of Romans deals with a whole raft of issues that we must realize in order to understand how to live by faith. When we give our hearts, our wills, our all to God, this is when we begin the process.

The Lord came to Abraham and said, "Abraham, get up and leave home; get out of town and go to the land I will show you." Look at Abraham's response. **"By faith Abraham, when called to go to a place he would later receive as his inheritance, obeyed and went, even though he did not know where he was going."**[1]

Living by faith is a constant daily experience of surrendering our wills to what the Holy Spirit says to us. The Holy Spirit is the One who guides us and nags us into being willing to do what Abraham did.

Now, look at what the Bible says in Romans 8:7. **"The mind governed by the flesh is hostile to God."** The word enmity was used earlier. Hostility and enmity are cousins. They are related.

The verse continues, **"It does not submit to God's law, nor can it do so."** This verse, unequivocally, says that those controlled by the sinful nature cannot, cannot, cannot... please God.

*Sinai Story*

At Mount Sinai, the most wonderful and amazing display of God's authority and power that mankind has ever witnessed took place!

About two million Hebrew slaves stood around this mountain on ground that was shaking. The quaking, flames of fire, and billowing smoke displayed a manifestation of God's majesty that mankind has not witnessed since! Picture in your mind how frightening this must have been. It was so frightening the Israelites literally trembled. They said, "Moses go and talk to Him; we're scared to death of Him." And so Moses climbed the mountain, then came back down and gave them the report

---

[1] Hebrews 11:8

God had sent. After Moses read God's response, they replied "All that God has said we will do." In their carnal state they thought they could do all that God wanted; but being awed into submission is no substitute for transforming grace.[1]

Think about it. In the days of Noah, if God had wanted to scare everybody into the ark and save the world, He need only to have left the door of the ark open until after it began to rain. God could have saved the entire world out of fear if salvation came by fear; but salvation comes by faith or it doesn't come at all!

The reason this is so important and I'm hammering on it so heavily, is that, when we get to Revelation's story at the time of the end, we are going to see that living by faith is essential.

God is going to cut off all of our food supply. He's going to cut off all of our ability to sustain ourselves. Everybody who receives the mark of the beast will do so because we cannot support ourselves without it.

God has designed an experience for the human race to see who will live by faith. Then we will see, not who is religious, not who knows their Bible and quotes the most text, not who is pious and who isn't. What we will see is, who can live by faith! That's what counts. It will be all that matters.

Understand, if you are willing to go and be and do as God directs, you will be in direct confrontation with the world on a daily basis, because the offspring of the serpent are hostile to the offspring of the woman.

### Shadrach, Meshach, and Abednego

One of the most wonderful faith stories in the Bible is found in Daniel 3. When the three young Hebrews stood on the plain of Dura, the great golden image had been erected and towered before them.

At the sound of the music, everybody was to come and bow down and express loyalty and allegiance to the king of Babylon.

---

[1] Exodus 20 explains details which happen in Exodus 19.

All of the satraps, princes, and governors: everybody who was anybody in Nebuchadnezzar's kingdom, were there.

But when the music sounded, Shadrach, Meshach, and Abednego stood erect. I imagine those three men stood out like a white dot on a black screen.

If you had been there that afternoon, would you have said to your two buddies, "I think this would be a good time for a word of prayer; let's kneel and pray for the king, then we won't be noticed and this whole thing will blow over."

Would you have had a thought like that? Have you ever compromised because of embarrassment? Sure, we all have.

To be willing to die for principle is foreign to our human nature unless we have been transformed by the power of God.

When the trumpets sounded and everybody knelt down, these three young man said, "God has commanded that we are not to bow down to any image," and they remained standing!

Their test of faith was intense. For people who live at the end of time, the test of faith will be just as intense and revealing.

In the end-time everyone will have to put faith either in the lamb-like beast—the devil—or, in the Lamb—the Son of God.

The world will have a choice: Lucifer or Christ.

The playing field will be the same. Only the master we choose to worship will make the difference.

The Bible says the sinful mind is hostile to God. This is why those controlled by the sinful nature cannot please God. This is why Cain killed Abel; he was in hostility toward God. Read Hebrews 11:4 and notice what the Bible says about Abel. **"By faith Abel brought God a better offering than Cain did."** And he did this by faith.

I am still describing two kinds of righteousness. Abel did what God required (kind two). He brought the right kind of offering at the right time. And in response to his faithfulness, God credited His own righteousness to Abel (kind one). God justified him.

Now, Jesus had not even lived on Earth yet and His righteousness had not been demonstrated, but by faith Abel was saved on the credit card plan. He was saved on the idea that, later, the price for sin would be paid. God reckoned Abel as righteous even though Abel had a fallen nature just like Cain. It was his living by faith that made the difference.

God gives us something that we cannot achieve, we cannot create, we cannot attain, and He gives it to us as a gift. But I can tell you, He will only give it when we surrender all. That's what living by faith is.

In God's economy, He requires a life for life, an eye for eye, a tooth for tooth. In God's equilibrium of justice, the eye of one is as valuable as the eye of another. The life of one is as valuable as the life of another.

When Noah came off the ark in Genesis 9:6, it was God who gave Noah the idea and revelation of capital punishment. God said, "If anyone kills another man, by man shall that murderer be put to death." This is what life for life means. You can see in the verse that God invented capital punishment. And He did so as a deterrent (detergent) to crime; because when people understand that the life of another is as precious as their own, they think twice about their actions.

*A Real Influencer*

What happens with sin and what is happening in schools today is that kids, who have been filled with thousands of hours of television and foolishness and murder and violence and evil of every sort, have no realization of the value of another life. Our society today is proof of what inevitably happens when this is prevalent.

The average child who reaches college today will have spent, I am told, more than 10,000 hours watching television. 10,000 hours! This is the same amount of time Gladwell, in his book *Outliers*, says is required to become a phenom or expert in a field. It's called the 10,000-hour rule. The Bible just says that *by beholding we become changed.* I believe that.

But what goes on in Hollywood and what happens on television is basically appealing to the carnal nature. And because the Bible says, "Our carnal nature is hostile toward God," my question is, how can we sit there and watch that stuff and be entertained by it, when it's contrary to everything that the Spirit of God leads us to love?

Jesus said, except a man be born again he cannot enter heaven. And the reason he cannot get into heaven is because he is unwilling to do God's will.

My prayer is, "Lord, make me willing. Lord, make me a servant. Lord, make me open to whatever you would have me do."

I never dreamed I would be preaching and writing books. It's the last thing on Earth I ever wanted to do. But when God calls, we go. When God commands, we obey.

Not to establish righteousness. We cannot establish our own righteousness. We are sinners and condemned from the start. But with the Holy Spirit's help and enabling, we can live by faith.

And because I have chosen—as far as I know—to live by faith, I have the assurance of the righteousness of Jesus. We all have it, because God can do anything!

Go to Romans 3:21–24 which says, **"But now apart from the law the righteousness of God has been made known** [in Christ's life], **to which the Law and the Prophets testify.** [This is a righteousness that has nothing to do with my compliance to law. This is talking about the righteousness of God.] **This righteousness is given through faith in Jesus Christ to all who believe. There is no difference between Jew and Gentile, for all have sinned and fall short of the glory of God, and all are justified freely by his grace through the redemption that came by Christ Jesus."**

Notice the words *Justified Freely*!

Let me tell you in practical terms what this meant to me

when it finally sunk in. I came to understand that, no matter how hard I try to conform my life to God's will, because I am a sinner, I'm still pretty repugnant in God's sight.

Even if I live the next 30 years and die at the age of 100 without committing any sin, I'm still a sinner; and the wages of sin is death by execution.

What I am trying to get you to understand and see in the good news of the gospel is, we don't have to perish. If we're willing to live by faith, God will give His righteousness to each of us, absolutely free.

The reason this is so crucial, and the reason salvation comes by faith and faith alone is because, to live with God, you can only do so and be happy, living by faith.

Let me explain that.

God is infinite, omnipotent, omniscient, and He does things in one hour that will take us 10,000 years to understand. So how can we live with Him, how do we get along with Him, until we understand Him?

There is only one way—by faith.

This is the same concept in which big financial arrangements are conducted. Contracts are entered into in good faith believing that each party has a mutual interest and good faith to see that it is consummated. It's called a good-faith contract. No matter how much language, no matter how many pages you write, no matter what all the language may declare, if it is not in good faith, it is no contract at all.

The whole idea is that we can only live with God throughout eternity and be happy with Him, if we live by faith. That means we have to accept that everything He does is righteous.

God can do no wrong.

He understands each one of us as individuals and has a plan and a purpose for us. He has an assignment for us, and if we are not willing to go and be and do that assignment here in this short span of time on Earth, it will be hell to live with Him in heaven for millions of years doing something we do not want to be doing.

The angels that stayed in heaven and fought against Lucifer and his angels actually stayed by faith. They did not understand (in its entirety) the nature and the enormity of sin. The flower of sin had not bloomed yet so that all of its details could be seen and understood.

The two-thirds of the angels that remained in heaven, stayed and were saved by faith. And likewise, the inhabitants of Earth who are saved will be saved by faith.

But there is one difference.

The angels were already in their holiest state and decided to stay with God. You and I are fallen. We are under the curse of sin. We humans have the propensity to do wrong; it's in our nature. But Jesus says, "Look, if you are willing to live by faith, I will give you My righteousness."

In Romans 4:1–3, Paul says, **"What then shall we say that Abraham, our forefather according to the flesh, discovered in this matter? If, in fact, Abraham was justified by works, he had something to boast about—but not before God."**

God is saying, "Okay you did a good job; I like you enough that I am going to keep you."[1]

Look closely at what the Scripture says, **"Abraham believed God, and it was credited to him as righteousness."** Credited—it was put over his life—he didn't earn it.

Romans 4:4–5, **"Now to the one who works, wages are not credited as a gift but as an obligation. However, to the one who does not work but trusts God who justifies the ungodly, their faith is credited as righteousness."**

Who is this talking about? The ungodly—the wicked!

Jesus told the Pharisees, "The prostitutes, the pimps, the drug pushers—the lowlife of creation—will enter heaven

---

[1] Abraham is the first man in the Bible to be called a prophet, and he lied twice in Egypt about his wife.

before you do."[1] This is because God justifies the wicked! If He didn't, He wouldn't justify any of us.

The truth is, we are all wicked. Jeremiah 17:9 says, **"The human heart is the most deceitful of all things, and desperately wicked. Who really knows how bad it is?"** (NLT)

Now look at Romans 4:18. The Bible says, **"Against all hope, Abraham in hope believed and so became the father of many nations, just as it had been said to him, 'So shall your offspring be.'"**

God had told Abraham that he would be the father of many nations. Abraham is old; his body is dead. This is before Viagra.

Against all HOPE!

Abraham is a human being. You have to understand the human side of the equation. What God was talking about made no sense. It didn't seem possible.

Notice what Romans 4:19 says, **"Without weakening in his faith, he faced the fact that his body was as good as dead—since he was about a hundred years old—and that Sarah's womb was also dead."**

Yet, in Romans 4:20 it says about Abraham, **"Yet he did not waver through unbelief regarding the promise of God, but was strengthened in his faith and gave glory to God."**

Wow, what a man! How would you describe a man that would look at himself and say, "God, this is impossible," but when he would look at God, he would say to the Lord, "With you Lord all things are possible, this is nothing"? This is a man of faith!

And soon after this, Abraham and Sarah conceived and brought forth the child God had promised.

Incidentally, I had a lady come over to me after a seminar and say, "You know, when the Lord fixed Abraham, He really fixed him good. Because after Sarah died, Abraham remarried and had several more children." This is another example that

---
[1] Luke 14:16–23

with God all things are possible. Faith demands it.

*Fiery Furnace Story*

Here is the problem. Daniel 3:16–18 says, **"Shadrach, Me-shach and Abednego replied to him, 'King Nebuchadnezzar, we do not need to defend ourselves before you in this matter. If we are thrown into the blazing furnace, the God we serve is able to deliver us from it, and he will deliver us from Your Majesty's hand. But even if he does not, we want you to know, Your Majesty, that we will not serve your gods or worship the image of gold you have set up.'"** Then, Nebuchadnezzar was furious. To be talked to like this in front of everybody who was anybody. Nebuchadnezzar had no option but to destroy these three men. His authority was at stake.

I like the way the King James Version states verse 19, **"and the form of his visage was changed against Shadrach, Me-shach, and Abednego,"** which means in plain English, he was embarrassed. I'm sure his face turned red. His blood pressure probably hit 220 over 150. Sweat must have broken out all over his body.

To be INSULTED like this!

And so, the Bible says, **"He ordered the furnace heated seven times hotter than usual and commanded some of the strongest soldiers in his army to tie up Shadrach, Meshach and Abednego and throw them into the blazing furnace."** And, you know the rest of the story.

What is so neat about this story is that because of the faith of these three young men, when all the satraps and princes, the governors and all of the lieutenants went back home, they told their friends and families: "We have seen the most amazing THING! Sure, we saw that big golden statue, but that's nothing. Let me tell you what we SAW! We saw the God of the Hebrews save three young men who defied the king! And we know the fire was hot, we know this was no show of smoke and mir-rors, because it killed the strongest of Nebuchadnezzar's army throwing them into the furnace. And then the three Hebrews' God came and stood in their midst. We saw it with our own eyes. Oh, what a GOD—What a God!"

I want to close this chapter with this thought: The only way God can reveal His magnificent greatness is through those who live by faith. There is no other way. Words cannot do it, or the silver-tongued orators would have finished the work long ago.

God can only demonstrate His magnificence and His glory and His power through those who are willing to live by faith. And if you are like Abraham and fully persuaded that God can do whatever He wants, even though your body may be dead, and you can go on your way with full assurance and confidence that God will do all He has said, you have no reason to have any fear. The only thing we have to fear is that we will forget how God has blessed us and led us in the past.

Dear reader, the righteousness that God offers is nothing we can produce. If we could produce it, then Jesus need not have come to Earth and died. He offers us His life, He will reckon us as though we have no sin, if we will only accept it and live by faith.

*A day is coming when the righteousness of Christ is going to be given to us.*

# CHAPTER 2

――――――

# Heirs of Abraham

I want to begin this chapter with a question we all need to consider. Why would any Christian want to be an heir of Abraham?

Notice what Galatians 3:28 says, **"There is neither Jew nor Gentile, neither slave nor free, nor is there male and female, for you are all one in Christ Jesus."** This verse says that Christ has brought an end to the distinctions among human beings. In Christ, we are one. There is neither Jew, there is neither Gentile.

Now, notice the next verse, **"If you belong to Christ, then you are Abraham's seed, and heirs according to the promise."** What was promised to Abraham, and why is it a big deal?

It's important because, as the verse indicates, if I am in Jesus, then I am actually an heir of all that was promised to Abraham.

The word SEED in the Greek is SPERMA from which we get the word Sperm. This term is expressing the origin of life. It means, IF you are Abraham's offspring, God reckons you as a son or daughter of Abraham, which brings us back to the opening question.

Many Christians today are totally confused about the distinction between Jew and Gentile. In fact, there is an entire eschatology of end-time events built around a set of circumstances for Christians and another for Jews.

It's amazing this kind of theological construct gets put forward when the Bible clearly says, in plain Greek, that in Christ there is NO distinction. **"There is neither Jew nor Gentile, neither slave nor free, nor is there male and female, for you are all one in Christ Jesus."**

Now, what is coming to Abraham and why is it so important? Keep reading. I'll show you.

*Law Before Mount Sinai*

In the previous chapter, I wrote about Cain. A couple more points are necessary because I frequently hear that prior to Mount Sinai, when God gave the Ten Commandments, there was no law. The whole premise behind this idea is that Christians need to find a way to justify lawlessness.

In Genesis 4 when Cain killed Abel, God said to Cain, **"If you do what is right, will you not be accepted?"** The word *right* implies that there is a *wrong*, although the text doesn't say so explicitly.

You will notice, if you talk with enough people, that there are two types of personalities who study the Bible. There are those who search it to defend what they want to believe, and those who study it to see what it says. Those who like to use proof texts use the Bible to defend what they want to believe. They want one verse that states everything they need to know. But those who study the Bible to see what it says want to look at the whole story to understand the ways of God. There is a profound difference in the two approaches.

Keep in mind, this is God speaking. **"If you do what is right, will you not be accepted?"** God is talking to Cain about his offering because he brought fruit instead of a lamb.

God continues, **"But if you do not do what is right, sin..."** Notice the word SIN. What does the presence of sin require? LAW...because where there is no law there is no sin.[1] If there is no speed limit, you cannot break the speed limit.

God continues speaking to Cain. **"Sin is crouching at your door [Cain]; it desires to have you, but you must rule over it."** Clearly, this verse indicates there was a knowledge of sin, which means there was also the presence of law.

The reason I am making this point so strenuously is that for 2,000 years—from Creation to Mount Sinai—the laws of God were written in the hearts of the people. The knowledge of God's law was conveyed orally from generation to generation. They were not written on tablets of stone at that time. However, a time is coming when God is again going to write His laws and ways in the hearts and minds of His people.

Now, you may say, "Wait a minute, has He not already done that? When you are born again, does He not write His laws and ways into our hearts?" The answer to that is a partial "Yes." Allow me to explain.

Notice in Drawing 2.1 the illustration of a book. When LARRY gave his life to Christ, Jesus covered him with His righteous life; and when the Father looks at Larry, He sees him JUST or justified. This means *just as though he never sinned,* because God is seeing the righteousness of Christ which covers Larry.

### Imputed / Imparted

This process, in theological terms, is called Imputed Righteousness. The word imputed is a legal term that simply means to reckon something as though it were; to look at Larry as though he were actually sinless even though, in reality, he's not. In a crude way it's like having a Power of Attorney.

When you have power of attorney, you have the right to

---

[1] Romans 5:13

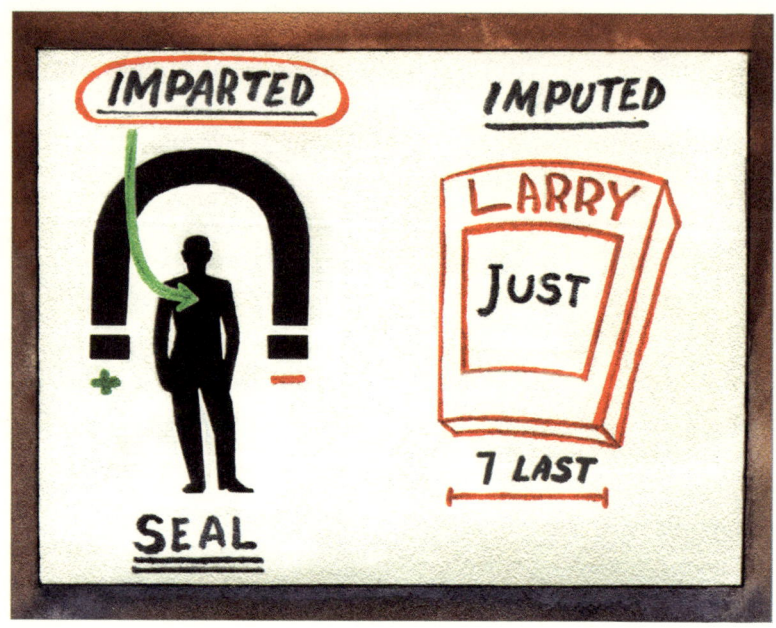

Drawing 2.1

conduct business on behalf of someone else; to sell their things or sign for them and conduct their business even though you are not actually that person. The law is ascribing authority to you to do business on behalf of someone else.

Imputing is a well-known legal expression, and it is used by theologians because that is, legally, exactly what is happening.

Larry is a sinner—he has violated the law—but by accepting Christ and living by faith, the righteousness of Christ is imputed or assigned to him. And when the Father looks at Larry, He sees him just as though he never sinned.

In the judgment of human beings, there is only one question asked: Is this person covered with the righteousness of Christ or not? Can you think of any reason to ask another question? No. Being covered by Christ's righteousness is the only thing that matters.

Now, the day is coming when the righteousness of Christ is going to be *imparted*. The two terms, *imputed* and *imparted*, are very different. We've already defined imputed, now let me explain what imparted means.

We need to understand the difference so that as we work our way from Genesis to Revelation, the whole story fits together harmoniously.

Look at Drawing 2.1 again and see if my explanation makes sense.

When Adam and Eve were created, they were attracted, naturally, to righteousness. They had a propensity for righteousness. When they were created, God put right doing within them.

This is depicted as a giant magnet having polls north and south; righteousness is represented as positive and sin as negative.

Because Adam and Eve were predisposed toward right doing, it was difficult for them to do evil. It was not normal. It was not natural. It was not easy. Evil was something that had to be done intentionally and defiantly, and that is what made the sin of Adam so grievous; he knew better but did it anyway.

Now Eve was deceived, and Paul never forgave her for that. You can see evidence of this in his writings.

When Adam and Eve sinned, their natures changed and they became attracted to wrongdoing. We can thank Adam and Eve for passing along to us that curse.

Now, when a person becomes born again, God puts into that person an understanding and love for right doing, but the nature itself is still carnal.

When you read Romans 7, you quickly understand that concept. Paul says in Romans 7:15, **"I do not understand what I do. For what I want to do I do not do, but what I hate I do."** He understood the struggle. We all can understand the struggle because it affects us all experientially.

When we become born again, the carnal nature is still there, and if we aren't watchful, it will rise up and bite us. In the born-again state, there is a spiritual nature and a carnal nature, and the two war against each other.

When Paul says, **"I die daily,"** his meaning is a reference to his carnal side. He's stating that his carnal desires have to be killed so that the Spirit can have dominion in his body.

Look at Drawing 2.1 again. A day is coming when the righteousness of Christ will no longer be imputed. During the end-times, it will be imparted. But before that happens, God is going to test every human being on Earth. It is called the mark-of-the-beast test.

God wants to see who will live by faith. And those who live by faith—after they've heard the gospel, made a decision for it, and been tested as to their determination—God will seal them.

This sealing, described in Revelation, is the imparting of the righteousness of Christ. This is where He removes the propensity for wrong doing and puts us back in the condition that Adam and Eve were originally.

According to the American Bible Society, there are about five billion people who have never heard the name of Jesus! The good news is, during the outpouring of the Holy Spirit, (a relatively short period of time in the end-times) a most marvelous thing is going to happen. God is going to send an intense series of events throughout the world so anyone who has never heard the name of Jesus will have an opportunity to hear the gospel. Jesus said, **"And this gospel of the kingdom will be preached in the whole world as a testimony to all nations, and then the end will come."**

God is going to have 144,000 servants strategically placed all around the globe and they will, at the right time, proclaim the gospel. Everyone will hear and consider it, then make a decision for or against it. Everyone will be tested as to where they stand. And after having been tested, individuals will either be sealed or marked. There is no in between. And the neat thing is—those who are sealed—God gives them a new nature!

Turn to Hebrews 8:10-12 and notice what the Bible says. **"This is the covenant I will establish with the people of Israel after that time, declares the Lord."**

Covenant is the key word here.

**"I will put my laws in their minds and write them on their hearts. I will be their God, and they will be my people."**

Notice the significance of the next verse.

**"No longer will they teach their neighbor, or say to one another, 'Know the Lord.'"**

This means in heaven there will no evangelist. The need for evangelism will be over. In heaven, there will be no need for doctors and no need for preachers. Their work will be over. **"Because they will all know me, from the least of them to the greatest. For I will forgive their wickedness and will remember their sins no more."**

Hebrews 8:13 says, **"By calling this covenant 'new,' he has made the first one obsolete; and what is obsolete and outdated will soon disappear."**

Now, Paul recognized the new covenant had not been implemented yet; but he was waiting for it. He anticipated it. Paul knew that a new covenant is coming. And this new covenant is where God puts His laws into our minds and hearts. Once He does this, He will have children who are in full harmony with Him once again.

The problem today is, in our current state, although we can understand God's laws and something of His ways, we have a carnal nature which is in natural rebellion against God. It just comes with the baby. Warfare is going on inside us.

So, during the time period of the Great Tribulation, God is going to impart the righteousness of Christ to every heart that is willing to live by faith, and then He is going to make it stick. He is going to seal that decision in them so it can't get away!

The reason you put a seal on something is to secure it. This explains how the saints, who have been sealed and receive the imparted righteousness of Christ, will go through a short period of time between the close of God's mercy and the Second Coming, committing no sin. They will have no attraction for it! It will have been taken away because by faith God gives them—imparts to them, puts within them—the very righteousness of Christ. God is going to do for us what we cannot do for ourselves, and that thrills my soul!

The reason I'm explaining this before going into the next chapter is because one of the things promised to Abraham is the imparted righteousness of Christ. This is why we want to be an heir of Abraham; Christ's righteousness is what was promised to him.

The other thing promised to Abraham is the land. When we have the righteousness of Christ and we have the land, we are prepared to enjoy eternity.

### The Flood

Look at Genesis 6:5–6. This is during the time period of the flood. Notice what the Bible says, **"The Lord saw how great the wickedness of the human race had become."**

How can you have wickedness without law being present? You can't. Read the remainder of the verse closely.

**"The Lord saw how great the wickedness of the human race had become on the earth, and that every inclination of the thoughts of the human heart was only evil all the time."**

Sounds like today, doesn't it?

**"The Lord regretted that he had made human beings on the earth, and his heart was deeply troubled."** God understands pain. He was heartsick.

Prior to Mount Sinai, the law of God had not been written on tablets of stone because, in the beginning, God had written the law on the hearts of His children. And when God has written His laws into the hearts of His children, they have an understanding of right and wrong that transcends what is written on paper.

*Nature of Law*

In the United States, the government regulation to sell a head of cabbage, for example, requires more than 29,000 words. Yet, the Gettysburg Address was a mere 272 words.

(Some say 269, some say 272. Evidently the original copy had 269 words and Lincoln added 3 words while delivering the speech, thus the discrepancy.)

Why is it that America has such an enormous amount of laws, and Congress continues to write more each year? One simple explanation is because the nature of man longs to be free without restriction.

Conversely, it is the nature of government to restrict and restrain men to gain power for itself. Our founding fathers understood the nature of men and the nature of government. This is why the U.S. Constitution was written—to restrict government, not the people. But to ferret this out would take another book.

If you write a series of laws that leave any loophole, it is natural for the nature of man to want to be free. It is also natural for the carnal nature to find a loophole to circumvent any law that restricts man's will to do as he pleases.

In the United States, resting upon each one of us, are more than 24,000 laws. Someone once did the research and calculated the number, although the number increases each year.

These laws range from selling cabbage to drinking water; traffic and property taxes to manufacturing. And every time government creates a new law, the carnal nature starts looking for a loophole to get out from underneath the obligation to it.

So, Congress, trying to eliminate the loopholes, creates more laws and the situation gets worse and worse!

The Bible says in Genesis 6:5–8, **"The Lord saw how great the wickedness of the human race had become on the earth, and that every inclination of the thoughts of the human heart was only evil all the time. The Lord regretted that he had** made human beings on the earth, and his heart was deeply troubled. So the Lord said, 'I will wipe from the face of the earth the human race I have created.' [God is taking responsibility for wiping mankind off the Earth. He says,] 'The earth the human race I have created—and with them the animals, the birds and the creatures that move along the ground—for I regret that I have made them.' But Noah found favor in the eyes of the Lord."

The point I want to make is that God reached a limit when He said, "The land is so corrupt, the land is so vile, that I am going to wash it and cleanse it with water." It is known as the great deluge.

I am leading up to something here, and it is this: He cleansed the land the first time with water, He will cleanse the land the second time with fire. God is very interested in the land, and is called the 'Land Lord' for good reasons.

### Garden of Eden

When Adam and Eve sinned, they were driven from the garden because of sin's curse. In Genesis 3, toward the end of the chapter, God said "they could not live in the garden and have access to the tree of life; they had to go." So He expelled them from the garden.

When Cain killed Abel, notice what the Lord said to Cain in Genesis 4:12–15, "When you work the ground, it will no longer yield its crops for you. You will be a restless wanderer on the earth."

What kind of person was Cain? A farmer—he worked the ground. And to tell a farmer that the land would no longer bear crops for him, that he could no longer raise grass or anything else, was to deprive him of his whole livelihood.

God said, "'You will be a restless wanderer on the earth.' Cain said to the Lord, 'My punishment is more than I can bear.'" This is like saying, *Just kill me and get it over with.* "Today, you are driving me from the land." Cain knew it was because of the curse of sin that he was being driven out. He was under a curse for having killed his brother. Incidentally, whenever a person is killed, the shed blood pollutes the land.

Cain continues, "**Today you are driving me from the land, and I will be hidden from your presence; I will be a restless wander on the earth, and whoever finds me will kill me.**"

Justice demanded it. Cain knew it.

"**But the Lord said to him, 'Not so; anyone who kills Cain will suffer vengeance seven times over.' Then the Lord put a mark on Cain so that no one who found him would kill him.**"

The Lord marked Cain and that mark was well understood.

The Bible doesn't say what the mark was, but it does tell us it was obvious, perhaps on his forehead or on his body so that it could be quickly seen.

Adam lived to be 930 years old. We don't know how old Cain lived to be; but he was the first born of Adam and the second man to live, so perhaps 900 years or close to it, given the longevity of that time. And when the Lord marked him it was known throughout the generations *"Do not harm that man."*

I think God allowed Cain to live because He wanted the flower of sin to bloom so that its mystery could be understood. We are born with a disposition toward evil and don't understand righteousness naturally. We are dead to it.

Until we are born again, we don't understand—nor like, nor appreciate, nor love—righteousness or the ways of God. We are in natural rebellion toward right doing. When we are born into rebellion, and that's all we know, we don't have anything to compare with righteousness.

The reason that God has allowed sin to exist from the beginning with Lucifer and the angels, is so the whole universe could understand that God's ways are right and best. Not because He is the almighty bully of the universe, but because by His wisdom and power and love and humility and suffering on Calvary, He has shown what the cost of sin really is, and demonstrated that His ways are righteous. I can love and serve a God like that!

So the Lord put a mark on Cain and he was driven—notice the phrase in verse 14—**"from the land."**

Americans do not appreciate *the land* quite like other nations. You, perhaps, are aware of the civil war between Bosnia, Croatia, and Serbia that destroyed Yugoslavia from 1991–2001. The big infighting there was all about land. The big fight in the Middle East today between the Jews and Arabs is all about land.

Americans do not understand the conflict because in our country we haven't had a struggle. No one wants California! If you want to buy a piece of it, people will gladly sell it to you.

When the Lord called Abraham, He wanted to give him a parcel of land. Go to Genesis 11:1. Time wise, this is approximately 100–150 years after the flood. Notice what the Bible says, **"Now the whole world had one language and a common speech."**

Remember, the whole world at this time had started with Noah and his wife, and his sons and their wives—eight people instead of two. "[The ark had landed on Mount Ararat, and] **As people moved eastward,** [to the more fertile spaces, and where the land was easier to obtain a living for both agriculture and for grazing,] **they found a plain in Shinar and settled there. They said to each other, 'Come, let us make bricks and bake them thoroughly.' They used brick instead of stone, and tar for mortar. Then they said, 'Come, let us build ourselves a city, with a tower that reaches to the heavens, so that we may make a name for ourselves and not be scattered over the face the whole earth."**

Some suggest that what this text is implying is that they were building the tower to show defiance toward God's promise that He would never destroy the world with a flood again. And the idea is that this tower was going to reach up to the heavens so that if another deluge ever came, they could all get above the flood and be secure and safe. That may well have been part of their thinking. However, I choose to look at the rest of the verse as to define their motive: "**So that we may make a name for ourselves and not be scattered over the face of the whole earth.**"

I believe their whole intention was to build a city, because mankind always resorts to some form of government. When you put two or more people together some type of government will inevitably occur. There will be a pecking order. Even gangs have government; one person is in charge; the tough rule over the weak. And what was going on at this tower is they had decided, "Let's stay together and not scatter out. Let's build a city and make a name for ourselves." "**But the Lord came down to see the city and the tower the people were building.**"[1]

The Lord had told Noah when he came off the ark to be fruitful and multiply. God wanted them to scatter over the face of the Earth. He wanted them to occupy it. But they said, "No, we're going to work together and build a city and protect ourselves from God."

Their decision not to comply is in direct rebellion to what God demanded of them. This building of a city is in direct opposition to the Word of God. That is how I interpret this.

So the Lord came down to see the city and the tower they were building; and Genesis 11:6–8 says, "**The Lord said, 'If as one people speaking the same language they have begun to do this, then nothing they plan to do will be impossible for them. Come, let us go down and confuse their language so they will not understand each other.' So the Lord scattered them from there over all the earth, and they stopped building the city.**"

Incidentally, the next verse tells us why the city was called Babel. Actually, the word Babel should be translated Babylon.

---

[1] Genesis 11:5

It is translated Babel consistently because, in the Hebrew, the word for confusion sounds like 'Babel,' but the actual word is Babylon. Now, I need to explain something.

In Drawing 2.2 is my rendition of a globe; and the X (without a circle around it) is Mount Ararat. Ararat is where Noah's ark came to rest. Then, as his family began to make their way southeastward, they found the verdant plain of Shinar which had fertile fields and water for irrigating the crops. It was a beautiful place. So they decided, "We'll make a city and settle here."

Remember, God had said just the opposite. He had said to be fruitful and multiply and scatter out. And finally, after He confused their languages, they had to scatter. They could no longer build the city. They could no longer work together. They could no longer live together.

What happened is, God created the languages and those who spoke a particular kind of language found each other, got together, and moved to another part of the earth. Every group did the same. This is why we have these people scattered into communities separated by languages. (X's inside circles with red barriers between them.)

How God did that, I'm not quite sure. He may have done it by family so that every member spoke the same language. He may have done it by personality type; there is no record of exactly how. But I can tell you this, two important things happened every time a group of people formed: A certain genetic pool became present, and all genetic characteristics of these individuals defined the dominant traits their offspring would eventually display. That's why we have genetic pools produced by the various groups of people.

### Earth Divided

The Bible says in Genesis 10:25, **"Two sons were born to Eber. One was named Peleg because in his time the earth was divided."**

*Drawing 2.2*

After these groups were formed and had moved away from each other, God pulled the land apart and put each group on its own continent. This is how we have the nations of the Earth and the unique characteristics that make up the genetic pool of each nation, today.

When you look at the globe, you can easily see how Africa would fit between North and South America. National Geographic has done a number of presentations on how the continents drifted apart. It's called the Continental Drift theory. I call it the continental movement fact. God just did it! This is the reason we have kangaroos in Australia. Kangaroos liked a certain group of people and when God pulled the continents apart—and that land mass was pulled away—they went with them! That is how we have animals in places around the Earth that are unique to those places.

Incidentally, Nature magazine—the leading publication on what is happening in geoscience—took a model of the Earth and moved all the continents back together into one land mass.

Notice the center of Drawing 2.2 for a visual of what the geoscientists did. In the illustration, all seven continents (red circles) are put back into one land mass. These geoscientists then looked for asteroid impacts that had occurred on the same latitude. They found five. I've drawn them as X's.

What was prompting this investigation is that in July 1994, when Shoemaker-Levy 9 plowed into Jupiter, it left the same type of footprint. Shoemaker-Levy 9 was a series of twenty-one comet fragments. One comet had broken into what was called the *string of pearls*, and as the planet rotated on its axis, the comet fragments came in and hit in a dot, dot, dot, kind of impact pattern and created a telltale footprint. This is illustrated on the right-hand side of Drawing 2.2.

The scientists wondered, if Earth's continents were brought back together as one land mass, whether there would be enough evidence to demonstrate that asteroid impacts had brought about the splitting up of Earth's continents.

Well—surprise, surprise! When they pulled it all together, they found five impacts (middle drawing) that lie on the same latitude. The two that are a little off are not statistically significant because things could be arranged a bit differently depending on how the separation occurred.

I believe the flood was caused by an asteroid impact. And Studies done at Berkeley, NASA, and a number of other agencies, can easily produce the modeling to show that the flood could have been caused by such a cataclysmic event.

Now, I don't doubt that God uses natural things to bring about natural disasters. I am not opposed to that idea at all. The point I'm leading up to should become clear from the next verse. So keep in mind that, once upon a time, this planet was a single land mass where all people spoke one language. Then, God confused the languages and pulled the world apart.

In Acts 17:18-26, Paul is in Athens. He is speaking to the

philosophers there—the Stoics and Epicureans—and they say, "Well, let's hear what this babbler has to say." They thought Paul was talking nonsense.

Paul then turns to them and says, "[Listen, what I have come to tell you is this: Gentlemen,] **from one man he made all the nations, that they should inhabit the whole earth; and he marked out their appointed times in history and the boundaries of their lands. God did this so that they would seek him and perhaps reach out for him and find him, though he is not far from any one of us.**"

This verse says it was by God's sovereign authority and omnipotent power that He pulled the globe apart and put every person in the exact place He wanted them. He placed great bodies of water, great mountain ranges, and various language barriers to keep groups of people separate while filling the globe.

Now, if God did that, then wouldn't it be fair to say that His salvation is open and generously available to all and has always been? Absolutely! We are saved by FAITH. There will be many resurrected, many rescued, many redeemed, who have never heard the name of Jesus but will inherit eternal life!

This means there are many Moslems, many Jews, many Catholics, many Hindus, many Protestants, many heathen, who went to their graves never knowing or understanding the ways and wonderful truths about God, yet will receive salvation. Such is the generosity of God!

In Ephesians 2:8-9, Paul says, **"For it is by grace you have been saved, through faith—and this is not from yourselves, it is the gift of God—not by works, so that no one can boast."**

Now, there is a backstory that goes with what Paul is saying.

Notice in Drawing 2.3 there is a black horizontal time line. The green vertical line represents the time period of the Flood. The orange vertical line represents the time period of the Tower of Babel.

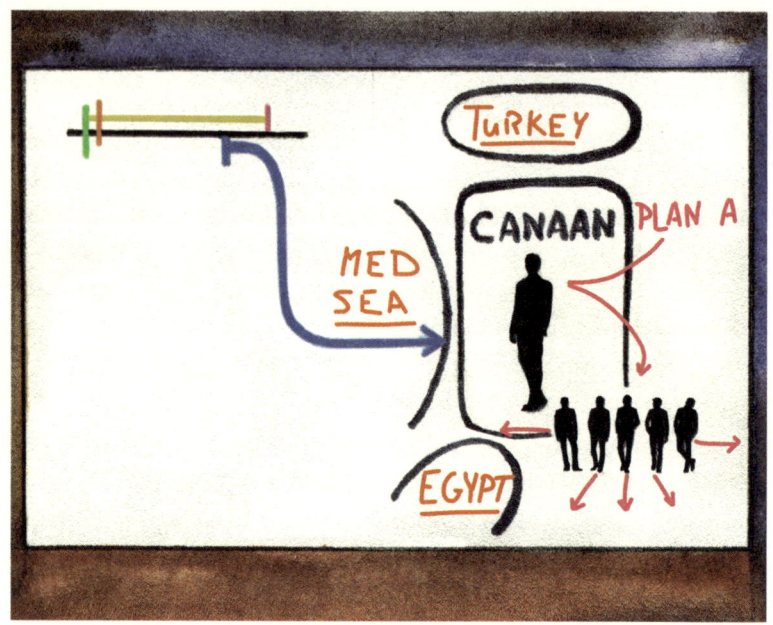

*Drawing 2.3*

Noah lived 350 years after the Flood and died at the age of 950; the pink vertical line represents this date. About 60 years before Noah died, God called Abraham to leave his home. The blue vertical line is when Abraham is called.

Noah and Abraham overlap each other; they lived briefly at the same time. Abraham was in Ur when God called him. At the time, Ur was in Babylon. Today, we call it Iraq.

Well, 100 years after the flood, Abraham was apparently in the group of people who were speaking a certain language that end up in the area of Babylon. And God called Abraham out of Babylon to a land that He would show him.

When God called Abraham to leave home, the Bible says, "Abraham left home not knowing where he was going."[1] The blue meandering line represents Abraham's trek. This is reminiscent of my traveling to certain places to conduct seminars. When you've never been to a certain place before, it's kind of

---

[1] Hebrews 11:8

hard to get there sometimes. The point is that after the Flood, after the cleansing and purging of the land of all the people, God sets out to do something with the land.

Jump to Genesis 12:1, "**The Lord had said to Abram, 'Go from your country, your people and your father's household to the land I will show you. I will make you into a great nation, and I will bless you; I will make your name great, and you will be a blessing. I will bless those who bless you,** and whoever curses you [I'll beat 'em up for you] **I will curse; and all peoples on earth** [ALL people] **will be blessed through you.'**"

At this time, Abraham had a very primitive religion. His knowledge of God was sufficient enough that God recognized he was a man of faith, but Abraham's religion was quite primitive. Nevertheless, God called him, educated him, refined him, ennobled him, and made him a great man and the father of a great nation.

The Bible says, "**And all peoples on earth will be blessed through you.**" Think of this in global terms. "**So Abram went, as the Lord had told him; and Lot went with him. Abram was seventy-five years old** [just about old enough to understand right from wrong] **when he set out from Harran. He took his wife Sarai, his nephew Lot, all the possessions they had accumulated and the people they had acquired in Harran, and they set out for the land of Canaan, and they arrived there.**"[1] It probably took nine to twelve months to get there.

Continuing with verses 6-7, "**Abram traveled through the land as far as the site of the great tree of Moreh at Shechem. At that time the Canaanites were in the land. The Lord appeared to Abram and said, 'To your offspring I will give this land.'**"

Notice the box drawn on the right-hand side of Drawing 2.3. This represents what we, today, understand to be the land of Canaan.

---

[1] Genesis 12:4–5

God called Abraham out of Babylon and took him over to the western part of the peninsula. You can see how the great Mediterranean Sea is to the west; Egypt is to the south; and Turkey is to the north.

The Lord continues, "**'To your offspring I will give this land.' So he built an altar there to the Lord, who had appeared to him.**"[1] Notice what Paul says in Hebrews 11:8 about Abram's experience, "**By faith Abraham, when called to go to a place he would later receive as his inheritance.**"

Here we go, talking about inheritance now.

God is going to give him an inheritance, and the inheritance is the land. Hebrews continues, "[He] **obeyed and went, even though he did not know where he was going.**"

Sometimes when God calls us to do certain things, He doesn't tell us the end, the destination. This requires faith.

I want to impress upon you that during the coming Great Tribulation when people take a stand to do what is right—to honor God, to be loyal to Him, to obey Him—the only way they will be able to survive is through faith. And doing this is so foreign to human nature. What human nature likes is security—in terms of dollars.

Our society has all kinds of schemes to create financial security: Social Security, IRAs, Keogh plans, pensions, etc. We have all kinds of arrangements to protect ourselves and to provide for ourselves. And to walk away from that security is scary. It isn't natural. But when we walk by faith, we go when and where God says.

God said to Abraham, "Leave your house, your homeland, and go to the place that I will show you." The Bible says, "Even though he did not know where he was going, he went!"

Wow, what a man of faith!

God said, "I am going to give you a piece of ground and bless all the peoples of the world through you, and I am going

---

[1] Genesis 12:7

to make of you a great nation." The Bible says that, **"By faith he [Abraham] made his home in the promised land like a stranger in a foreign country."**[1] Because when he got there, the Canaanites were already there!

Understand that even though we walk the earth today, and even though others own it, and others have the authority and power and wealth of the world, God's children will inherit the Earth! Even though the Canaanites occupy it right now, they won't have it for long. God is going to give it to His children.

Let me try and explain what God's plan was and demonstrate it, so you can see in your mind's eye what His intentions were.

### Plan A / Plan B

Under *Plan A*, God had no intention, ever, of a second coming. There is no second coming in the Old Testament except for the book of Daniel, and Daniel's prophecy is a projection of what will take place at the end of time in *Plan B*. In God's original plan, *Plan A*, everything was setup to play out very differently.

In *Plan A*, God proposed to set up Abraham and his descendants as trustees of the gospel. God was going to start with a very beautiful piece of ground (Canaan), give it to a man of faith, and from this man of faith, have a whole house full of children who would also live by faith and fill the land. These children would then go throughout the world and tell of God's great love. And the day would eventually arrive when God would come down, enlarge the borders of Canaan, encompass the whole world, separate good from evil, and destroy evil. This is basically what the Old Testament is all about. I call it *Plan A*—God's original plan.

For the Old Testament promises to make sense, we must understand that God's original intent was that Abraham and his descendants were going to fulfill the plan by populating the

---

[1] Hebrews 11:9

Earth. Eventually the day would come when Messiah Himself would be born in the city of Jerusalem, and after having established the throne of David, king Gog of Magog would marshal his forces against Messiah, Messiah would finally destroy him, and evil would be done away with.

That is the story in a nutshell.

However, God's *Plan A* wasn't implemented because the children of Israel would not cooperate. They rebelled every step of the way. God intended to take them out of Egypt into the Promised Land, but they didn't get there because of rebellion. Israel refused to live by faith, so God killed them in the desert.

He restarted the process with multiple generations until, finally, Jesus came and God said, "Look, I am tired of the whole thing. I'm opening up the doors so that any person can be Abraham's offspring if he will receive Christ; because the promise I made to My friend Abraham still remains. I am going to give Abraham the Promised Land. I am going to give Abraham and all of his children what I intended from the very beginning. And those whose hearts are filled with rebellion and will not live by faith, and will not put faith and trust in Me, I don't want them in My land."[1]

*New World Order*

Hebrews 11:10 makes the point perfectly clear. **"For he [Abraham] was looking forward to the city with foundations, whose architect and builder is God."** Who has built the New Jerusalem? God! The reason there is a New Jerusalem is because the old one could not be used.

The Promised Land is not just a parcel of dirt called Canaan. The Promised Land that God is going to give Abraham is a new world! This will truly be THE New World Order!

The difference depends on which word you put the emphasis. Some people say, new WORLD order, and some say, NEW

---

[1] Genesis 32

*Drawing 2.4*

world order. This 'NEW WORLD order' is going to consist of a NEW EARTH and a NEW HEAVEN! And God is going to give it to Abraham's offspring.

Go to Revelation 7:9. This verse excites me!

**"After this I looked, and there before me was a great multitude that no one could count, from every nation, tribe, people and language, standing before the throne and before the Lamb. They were wearing white robes and were holding palm branches in their hands."**

Drawing 2.4 shows the time period of the Great Tribulation. The cloud represents the second coming when Jesus returns in clouds of glory, and Revelation 7:9 applies right afterward. You can see the pink arrow indicating this happens after the second coming.

John says, **"After this I looked, and there before me was a great multitude that no one could count."** I would say the word NUMBERLESS would be a fair summary. A great multitude!

Notice that the Bible says, they come **"from every nation, tribe, people and language."** It also says they are **"standing before the throne."** So this is obviously after the second coming, and this numberless crowd has come from everywhere!

The story is about everybody, everywhere **"standing before the throne and before the Lamb. They were wearing white robes."**

Interestingly, white robes have been given to them. What do the white robes represent? Revelation 19 says that the fine linen given to the saints is the righteousness of Christ! And they, the Bible says, **"were holding palm branches in their hands."** This suggests they had gained a victory. Palm branches always go with victory.

Revelation 7:10 says, **"And they cried out in a loud voice: 'Salvation belongs to our God, who sits on the throne, and to the Lamb.'"** This cry is significant. It is a statement of worship.

This great multitude that no one can count is standing around the throne saying, "Man, I made it because I was good enough to be here!"

Is that what they are saying? No.

Everyone standing before the throne is looking up at the Father and the Son, saying, "Salvation belongs to our God and His salvation was given to us as a gift."

Revelation 7:11–12 continues, **"All the angels were standing around the throne and around the elders and the four living creatures. They fell down on their faces before the throne and worshiped God, saying: 'Amen! <u>Praise</u> and <u>glory</u> and <u>wisdom</u> and <u>thanks</u> and <u>honor</u> and <u>power</u> and <u>strength</u> be to our God for ever and ever. Amen!'"** Did you notice that the seven attributes of God are underlined? **"Then one of the [twenty-four] elders asked me, '[John, this great crowd here, this numberless multitude coming from everywhere] These in white robes [holding the palm branches]—who are they, and where did they come from?' I [John] answered, 'Sir, you** know.' [This is a diplomatic way of saying, I don't know.] **And he said, 'These are they who have come out of the great tribulation; they have washed their robes and made them white in the blood of the Lamb.'"**

I want to make a point here for clarification. Consider that this crowd, this throng of people being discussed, is not the harvest of all people throughout history. This multitude is not from a group of people that started with Abel. This is a specific group of people that are unique to the time period of the Great Tribulation, indicated between the two blue vertical lines in Drawing 2.4.

The verse is referring to people that ONLY come out of the Great Tribulation. This tells me two important things:

> *1) That during the final days of Earth's history, when the power of God is poured out in the latter rain, the harvest is going to be incalculable. You cannot count numberless.*
>
> *2) What this means, in practical terms, is that our chance of being redeemed is very great.*

Understand the significance of this! If the story turned out that the number to be redeemed was only three, what would our hope be?

Rejoice about the word *numberless*! God is going to save a *numberless* multitude!

This means that what was promised to Abraham will be secure. God promised that old man, his descendants would be as numerous as the stars in the sky. If you've ever tried to count the stars you know you can't count them. There are just too many.

The significance of what this is saying is, all of us have a chance! This is a story about God opening the floodgates. He is going to make the threshold of salvation so low that any and all who wish to be saved, can be!

As we come to the end of the chapter, I want to leave you with something to think about as you think about Drawing 2.4.

I believe the final test of faith that is coming upon the world during the Great Tribulation will be a test of worship. I believe that the fourth commandment, God's Sabbath, is going to be a special object of contempt and a special object of affection—depending on your spiritual condition and position. The devil has set up a special contempt for the Sabbath because it honors our Creator.

During this time period, with the first angel's message (green color), God is going to send the command throughout the earth: "Worship God, the Creator of Heaven and Earth." God is going to see who will live by faith. Carefully understand the properties involved in this test.

If God required us to do something in order to be saved, it would be salvation by works. But of the Ten Commandments, the fourth commandment is the only one that requires us to do nothing at the right time each week. God commands His children under the most distressing circumstances—the threat of the loss of livelihood, home, clothing, food, shelter, even ridicule and embarrassment, everything—honor Me and I will see you through.

Now, He may see some of us through to death. He says, "If you are to perish, don't worry about it. If you are going into captivity, don't worry about it. I am with you always, even to the end of the world."[1] God is going to test our faith, and the threshold will be very low. The only question will be, will you step over onto His side?

A lot of Christians believe that God's holy Sabbath day was nailed to the cross. The next chapter is going to discuss this. Most Christians today are convinced that prior to the cross, there were Ten Commandments, and now there are nine.

And what most Christians justify is the illogical idea that the Ten Commandments were bad so God nailed them to the cross—did away with them—but then reinstated nine, leaving out the fourth.

---

[1] Revelation 13:10

There is a special contempt for the Sabbath.

Now, understand, keeping the Sabbath, or any other commandment, does not bring salvation. It can't. There are two kinds of righteousness: one that comes from God, and one that is produced by obedience. The one necessary for salvation has to come from God. But there is a relationship between God's Ten Commandments, faith, and righteousness, and in the next chapter I'll try to bring those things together.

I hope that after reading this far, you have a new appreciation for what it means to be an heir of Abraham. Abraham was promised the land and he was promised a new nature. If you plan to enjoy eternity, you're going to need both. And this is why every Christian should be thrilled with the promise of being a part of the family of Abraham.

Pray with me.

Oh Father in heaven, precious Jesus, thank you for the words of encouragement that we find in your Scripture. As we look at what you promised Abraham and what you intended to do through him, and we realize that now, through adoption, we can be an heir of Abraham through Christ. What a privilege you've bestowed upon us that we should be called your children. I pray that when you come in the clouds of glory, dear Jesus, that every one of us will be prepared and ready, and we'll stand together and say, "Surely this is our God and we have waited for Him and He will save us!" Remember us, oh Jesus, when you come into your kingdom for Thine is the power and the glory forever, amen.

*When you are born again, God
gives you special power to reach
beyond what you can humanly do.*

# CHAPTER 3

## The Gospel Message

The first chapter explained why our Lord chose four men to write the Gospels. He did so because one particular view is not adequate. I believe the same is true for righteousness by faith.

When Martin Luther was working on and translating the Bible into the German language, he had already discovered righteousness by faith. And when he came to the books of Hebrews, James, and Revelation, he would have left them out of the German version of the Bible had it not been for some of his associates. He hated those three books. He saw no practical value in them whatsoever.

That little factoid is interesting to me because it's a good example of the nature of man. No one person can surround and understand all that God is. He is infinite. We are far from it.

### Unilateral / Bilateral Covenants

To understand what God has planned for mankind, we must understand the difference between a unilateral covenant and a bilateral covenant. There is an important distinction between the two.

As shown in Drawing 3.1, unilateral means one sided. The Declaration of Independence is an example of a unilateral covenant. WE THE PEOPLE DECLARE is a unilateral statement. The declaration is not open for negotiation. It is not open for discussion. It is simply a statement of how things are going to be. No ifs, ands, or buts about it.

In Genesis 2:17, God placed a unilateral covenant upon Adam and Eve in the Garden of Eden. He said, **"For when you eat from it you will certainly die."** Notice that He doesn't ask how they feel about it. He simply states it is the way things are going to be.

The reason we call it a covenant, and also a law, is that it is perpetually in effect. So, even if Adam and Eve had borne offspring in the garden, they too would have been under the obligation of the unilateral covenant. Their offspring couldn't have eaten of that tree either. This unilateral covenant is God acting alone and simply declaring something to be.

The Ten Commandments also are a unilateral covenant. God spoke them and they're not open for negotiation. Whether we like them or dislike them, whether we accept them or reject them, is immaterial. They collectively are a unilateral covenant and were kept in a little box called the Ark of the Covenant, in the tabernacle.

There are a number of unilateral covenants in the Bible. Another excellent example is found in Genesis 9. After the flood when Noah came off the ark, God made a unilateral covenant with man and creatures. **"Never again will all life be destroyed by the waters of a flood."** God declared it and said, "I am going to put in the heavens the sign of the covenant and every time you see a rainbow, remember the covenant."

You should, by now, be able to see what a unilateral covenant means. This is important to understand, because later,

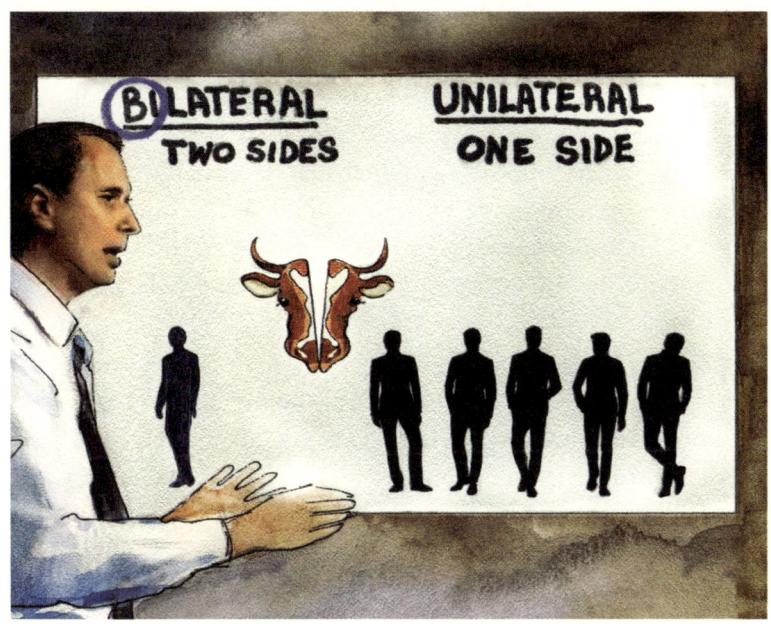

*Drawing 3.1*

we're going to see how it plays out on a much larger scale.

Now, let me describe a bilateral covenant. Bi means divided, or, having two sides. A bicycle has two wheels whereas a unicycle has one. You might say that a bilateral covenant requires the cooperation and mutual consent of at least two parties. For example, a marriage can be considered a bilateral covenant. It is perpetual for as long as either spouse shall live; this applies to both spouses.

A bilateral covenant requires the performance of both parties. In order for the covenant to remain intact, certain specifications within the covenant are stipulated. A bilateral covenant is always conditional; meaning that if one of the parties doesn't live up to whatever the terms of the covenant are, then the covenant is broken.

Not so with a unilateral covenant. You cannot break a unilateral covenant. You may violate it, you may ignore it, you may neglect it, you may refuse it—but this doesn't change a unilateral covenant. If we were to collectively act badly, do you think it would change whether God is going to send a flood upon the Earth again? No. In fact, if all people on Earth were to simultaneously be nasty and mean, God would not destroy the Earth with a flood again because a unilateral covenant cannot be broken, made null, or voided. What this is leading up to is, in understanding righteousness by faith, you have to understand the operation of covenants and how they relate to salvation.

Previously, I brought up the question, "Why would any Christian want to be an heir of Abraham?" Look at this text, **"If you belong to Christ, then you are Abraham's seed, and heirs according to the promise."**[1]

I want to demonstrate why I believe God made two covenants with Abraham: one is a unilateral covenant, the other a bilateral covenant. We must understand the distinction between the two types of covenants or we'll end up in Revelation with an eschatology that is totally confused and misses the point of what is being said.

In Genesis 12:1, when God called Abraham to leave his home, notice what the Bible says. **"The Lord had said to Abram, 'Go from your country, your people and your father's household to the land I will show you.'"** What God said to Abraham is unilateral. Abraham is about 75 years old. God had observed Abraham's life and knew he was a man with which a unilateral covenant could be made, because a unilateral covenant is an everlasting covenant when God makes it.

Notice what He said to Abraham in the following verses, **"I will make you into a great nation... I will make your name great and you will be a blessing. I will bless those who bless you, and whoever curses you I will curse; and all peoples on earth** [this means everybody, everywhere] **will be blessed through you."**[2]

---

[1] Galatians 3:29
[2] Genesis 12:2

In this verse God is making a universal, unilateral covenant with Abraham. Later, God made a bilateral covenant with him. **"The Lord said to Abram after Lot had parted from him, 'Look around from where you are, to the north and south, to the east and west. All the land that you see I will give to you and your offspring forever. I will make your offspring like the dust of the earth, so that if anyone could count the dust, then your offspring could be counted.'"[1]**

God is restating in verse 16 what He had already promised in an earlier verse. And He's saying this to a man who is childless. God continues, **"Go, walk through the length and breadth of the land, for I am giving it to you."[2]**

In Genesis 15:1–6, the covenant takes on a little different dimension. **"After this, the word of the Lord came to Abram in a vision: 'Do not be afraid, Abram. I am your shield, your very great reward.'"**

Abraham, in response, gets right to the point. "Lord, if you are my shield and my very great reward, how is it that I am still childless? How is it that I have no offspring? I am actually a pilgrim in this land because the people who occupy it are not willing to give it to me. I asked them...they said, 'No.'"

Abraham continues, **"Sovereign Lord, what can you give me since I remain childless and the one who will inherit my estate is Eliezer of Damascus? You have given me no children; so a servant in my household will be my heir." "Then the word of the Lord came to him: 'This man will not be your heir** [God just comes right out and says this is not going to happen!], **but a son who is your own flesh and blood will be your heir.' He took him outside and said, 'Look up at the sky and count the stars—if indeed you can count them.' Then he said to him, 'So shall your offspring be.'"**

I like verse 6 because it is so meaningful. **"Abram** [the baron, childless, homeless Abraham] **believed the Lord, and he**

---

[1] Genesis 13:14–16

[2] Genesis 13:17

**credited it to him as righteousness.**" This is what faith is in its most simplistic explanation. Faith is really no more complicated than that. Abraham believed God and His word, and the Lord credited that to him as righteousness.

Their conversation continued, "**He also said to him, 'I am the Lord, who brought you out of Ur of the Chaldeans to give you this land to take possession of it.' But Abram said, 'Sovereign Lord, how can I know that I will gain possession of it?'**"[1]

In verse 6, we read that "Abraham believed the Lord," but now he is asking: "How can I believe this… how will I know this… how can I be assured of this?"

The human mind needs and searches for understanding. It is part of the human composition to try and make sense of things we don't understand. Abraham wanted to know with some assurance: "How can I know that I'm going to get what you've promised?"

*Blood Covenants*

In the United States of America, we don't understand the ritual described in the following verses because it is not our practice to offer blood covenants. I will explain what they are and what is going on after we read a few relevant verses.

Genesis 15:9–16 says, "**So the Lord said to him, 'Bring me a heifer, a goat and a ram, each three years old, along with a dove and a young pigeon.'**" If you have studied the sanctuary, you should immediately recognize that these are the same five animals used in the sanctuary services.

"**Abram brought all these to him,** [and then he did something very strange. He] **cut them in two** [right down the middle as illustrated in Drawing 3.1] **and arranged the halves opposite each other; the birds, however, he did not cut in half. Then birds of prey came down on the carcasses, but Abram** [who is sitting by the carcasses] **drove them away. As the sun was setting, Abram fell into a deep sleep, and a thick and dreadful**

---

[1] Genesis 15:7–8

darkness came over him. **Then the Lord said to him, 'Know for certain that for four hundred years your descendants will be strangers in a country not their own and that they will be enslaved and mistreated there. But I will punish the nation they serve as slaves, and afterward they will come out with great possessions.'"**

God was predicting the Egyptian slavery Israel would encounter in the future. **"'You, however, [Abraham] will go to your ancestors in peace and be buried at a good old age. In the fourth generation your descendants will come back here, for the sin of the Amorites has not yet reached its full measure.'"**

Let me make a point about what we just read. God does not steal land from one body of people to give to another. He doesn't step in and say, "Away with you guys, I'm going to give this land to whomever I wish." God doesn't behave that way. He is not arbitrary. He gives all nations a period of time, and when they fill up their cup of inequity, He destroys them.

This is called the Full Cup Principle. This principle is why Babylon rose and fell. It is why Egypt, Assyria, Medo-Persia, Grecia, and Rome rose and fell. And it is why the United States has risen and is falling.

This shouldn't be too hard to understand.

God was saying to Abraham, "When the sin of the Amorites has reached full measure—when they have filled up their cup—the land will vomit them out, they will be destroyed, and I will bring you in to take their place."

Now, verse 17 is the part where things get strange. It continues from where the animals are lying on the ground. **"When the sun had set and darkness had fallen, a smoking firepot** [or what we would today call a skillet. The word censer in Hebrew means skillet. Someone is carrying this skillet along] **with a blazing torch** [and they] **appeared and passed between the pieces. On that day the Lord made a covenant with Abram** and said, 'To your descendants I give this land, from the Wadi of Egypt to the great river, the Euphrates.'"[1]

What do you suppose "walking between the pieces of the carcasses" is all about? What God was doing was entering into a blood covenant with Abraham.

A blood covenant is where two parties agree to be partners, and the only way to be released from this covenant is for one of them to die! Think of this as the most serious type of covenant that can be made between two parties.

The slaughter of the animals and the shedding of their blood is where this idea comes from; and one of the parties has to walk between the pieces to secure the agreement. In this case, Jesus walked through the pieces.

*Life for Life*

This covenant is built upon a concept that is used throughout the Old Testament, it is called judicial equilibrium. Judicial equilibrium is when we have an eye for an eye, tooth for tooth, and bruise for bruise. In God's economy, He always sees that judicial equilibrium is maintained. The sanctuary service clearly identifies how the system works.

Abraham knew he was going to be the father of a great nation. He knew that he had been chosen and God was going to give him a big parcel of ground. Abraham knew lots of things, but he also knew that he had no children. Eventually, Abraham and Sarah tried to help God fulfill His promise by bringing Hager into the picture. The Middle East is still dealing with the problems caused by their impatience.

Now, God came to Abraham a little later in Genesis 17 and told him things were not going to happen that way. Notice what Genesis 17:1 says, **"When Abram was ninety-nine years old, the Lord appeared to him and said, 'I am God Almighty; walk before me faithfully and be blameless.'"**

In other words, God is saying, "Abraham, I am calling you

---

[1] Genesis 15:17–18

to a higher standard of conduct than what you have been doing. You have messed up. You went down into Egypt and you lied to Abimelek about your wife because of your lack of faith. Now you have this son, Ishmael, because of lack of faith. Abraham, get your act together. I am God Almighty; when I make a promise, I am able to keep it. Walk before me and be blameless. Do what you know is right."

God continues, "**'I will make MY covenant between me and you and will greatly increase your numbers.' Abram fell facedown, and God said to him, 'As for me, this is my covenant with you: You will be the father of many nations.'**"[1]

Earlier, back in Chapter 12, God had said "**I will make you into a great nation,**" singular. But in chapter 17, God tells Abraham "**You will be the father of many nations,**" plural.

Abraham is the father of the Arabs. Ishmael, his firstborn, had twelve sons and they became twelve great nations. And today, according to the Muslim tradition, they consider Ishmael—not Mohammed—the founder of their faith. Mohammed was simply a prophet, but Ishmael is the father of the Muslim faith. Abraham, then, had another son named Isaac, and he, the Bible says, would be the progenitor through whom the promise would be carried. Since Abraham had messed up with Hagar and Ishmael, God is saying, "[Abraham, we are going to amend the covenant. Now you're going to be the father of many nations, not just one.] **No longer will you be called Abram; your name will be Abraham, for I have made you a father of many nations.**"

The difference between the names Abram and Abraham has to do with *inclusiveness* instead of *exclusiveness*. In Christ's time, the Jews thought of Abraham as their father not realizing that even by using his name they were using an inclusive name. Abraham is the father of many nations, not just one.

The Bible continues, "**'I will make you very fruitful; I will make nations of you, and kings [plural] will come from**

[1] Genesis 17:2–4

you. I will establish my covenant as an everlasting covenant between me and you and your descendants after you for the generations to come, to be your God and the God of your descendants after you. The whole land of Canaan, where you now reside as a foreigner, I will give as an everlasting possession to you and your descendants after you; and I will be their God.' Then God said to Abraham, 'As for you, you must keep my covenant, you and your descendants after you for the generations to come. This is my covenant with you and your descendants after you, the covenant you are to keep.'"[1]

The language here is a little confusing at first. You might think after reading this that the covenant is simply circumcision, but it isn't. **"Every male among you shall be circumcised. You [Abraham] are to undergo circumcision, and it will be the sign of the covenant between me and you."**[2]

Circumcision is the sign of the covenant, not the covenant itself. Bilateral covenants always have something in consideration as a sign of an agreement. Let me explain.

If you, as a parent, wish to give your car to your child and transfer the title from your name to his, most states require some amount of money ($25) as a consideration in order to make it a legal transfer of title. A covenant has to have a sign. There has to be something that goes with it, external from it, to verify its existence. So when you go down to the courthouse to transfer your car, that twenty-five dollar transfer fee is evidence that this is a legal transaction and that someone legally transferred this property from one person to another. You cannot have a contract without some kind of consideration.

When you buy a car or a house, they require a down payment; or at least they used to. Today with all of the monopoly money being printed, they may not require one, but historically, that has been the case.

God is giving Abraham circumcision as a sign of the

---

[1] Genesis 17:6–10
[2] Genesis 17:10–11

bilateral covenant; He did this because Abraham's descendants are going to be His chosen people as trustees of the gospel.

In Acts 13:47, when Paul was giving his defense, notice what he said: **"For this is what the Lord has commanded us** [referring to Jews or Israel]: **'I have made you a light for the Gentiles, that you may bring salvation to the ends of the earth.'"**

What was God's purpose in choosing the offspring of Abraham? What was the point of having special people on Earth? The verse says, **"I have made you a *light* for the Gentiles.** [Everyone who isn't a Jew]" There are only two kinds of people in the Jewish economy. There is the Jew on the one hand and everybody else on the other. That's all there is.

God is saying, "I have called you, I have made you, I have selected you to do this, because I loved Abraham. That man was such a man of faith that I wanted to have a whole raft of baby Abrahams going throughout the Earth, carrying the good news and telling people of my salvation. I have made you a 'light to the Gentiles' that you may bring the message of salvation to the ends of the Earth. This is your calling. This is why I chose you. This is why I've entered into a covenant with you. This is why—and the only reason why—you are special."

Remember, Moses told the people in Deuteronomy, "Listen you guys, don't think you're anything special. God didn't choose you because you are big and powerful; He didn't chose you because you are smart. The Lord knows you're hardheaded and obstinate. God chose you because He loved Abraham. Abraham was a man of faith and nothing pleases God like faith, and He chose you because He wanted you to be like Abraham."

Hebrews 11:6 says, **"Without faith it is impossible to please God."** Abraham pleased God. He upset God from time to time, but overall, Abraham was a man of enormous faith.

When God called Abraham to slay his only son on top of Mount Moriah, he was willing. And as Isaac lay there,

Abraham, with tears running down his face, said to him, "If necessary, God can raise you up." That is a statement of faith! Abraham had never seen a resurrection in his life, but he knew it was possible, for "with God all things are possible."[1] In Acts 13:48 the Bible says, **"When the Gentiles heard this** [the news that they could be part of God's family], **they were glad."**

Before proceeding, let me make one more point about circumcision being a sign. For obvious reasons, it isn't the kind of sign you casually flaunt!

*The Sanctuary*

In the little building called the *Sanctuary* were two rooms: The Holy Place and Most Holy Place. The Ark of the Covenant sat inside the Most Holy Place.

What was inside the Ark of the Covenant? The covenant!

And after the law was given, and Moses safely got down the mountain with the two tablets of the covenant and put them in the ark, no one got to see the law afterward. What was so important that God would leave heaven, come down to Mount Sinai, proclaim to Moses and write on stone, and then have it hidden so nobody would ever see it again?

The Bible never mentions anyone ever seeing the stone tablets of the covenant again. It could not be looked upon. In fact, when the Ark of the Covenant traveled, it was always shrouded in the drapery of the veil. They would carefully unhang the veil—the curtain that hung between the Holy and Most Holy places—and cover the ark when the camp moved from place to place. And the children of Israel, as they followed the ark, were required to stay two-thirds of a mile from the ark! Two-thirds of a mile is a long way on foot!

God hid His covenant because He wanted it written on their hearts and not on tablets of stone. They would have worshiped the tablets of stone, just as they had worshiped the golden calf, so God hid it from their sight.

---

[1] Matthew 19:26

In the same way, He chose a private part of Abraham and Ishmael to be circumcised because He wanted them to understand that their being chosen was all about what goes on inside, not outside.

God is using this act to symbolize circumcision of the heart because, when we are born, we come from the womb with a carnal nature; and until the Holy Spirit can crack its hard shell, the potential to be spiritual is hidden. Everybody has the potential for being spiritual, but not everyone opens up to let the Spirit in. And so God gave Abraham the sign of circumcision.

Notice what God said, "**As for you, you must keep my covenant, you and your descendants after you for the generations to come. This is my covenant with you and your descendants after you, the covenant you are to keep: Every male among you shall be circumcised. You are to undergo circumcision, and it will be the sign of the covenant between me and you. For the generations to come every male among you who is eight days old must be circumcised, including those born in your household or bought with money from a foreigner—those who are not your offspring. Whether born in your household or bought with your money, they must be circumcised. My covenant in your flesh is to be an everlasting covenant.**"[1]

What kind of covenant? Everlasting!

Verse 14, "**Any uncircumcised male, who has not been circumcised in the flesh, will be cut off** [pun intended] **from his people; he has broken my covenant.**"

The reason I am hammering on this is because in Acts 15, a big argument had broken out among the new believers. Some were saying "circumcision is necessary to be saved," others were saying "not so."

Genesis 17:12–14 are the verses in dispute. I hope you're beginning to see that there is justification for having broken this everlasting blood covenant.

---

[1] Genesis 17:9–13

In Exodus 19:3–6, we have progressed about 400 years from the time of Abraham all the way down to Mount Sinai. Carefully consider what is stated in the following four verses, especially the conditional nature of what is said.

**"Then Moses went up to God, and the Lord called to him from the mountain and said, 'This is what you are to say to the descendants of Jacob and what you are to tell the people of Israel: "You yourselves have seen what I did to Egypt, and how I carried you on eagles' wings and brought you to myself. Now [the most dreaded word in the English language... IF...] if you obey me fully and keep my covenant, then out of all nations you will be my treasured possession. Although the whole Earth is mine, you will be for me a kingdom of priests and a holy nation." These are the words you are to speak to the Israelites.'"**

What does God mean by priests?

The definition of a priest is someone who is appointed by God to serve between God and man.

And whom did He choose out of the house of Israel to serve Him as priests? The descendants of Levi.

And why did He choose the descendants of Levi? Because they did not worship the calf; they defended and upheld the Holy name of God and He chose them as the ones He wanted close to Him.

God intended the whole nation of Israel should demonstrate this same kind of loyalty as a kingdom of priests! And that calling and opportunity was predicated on "If you do what I command."

Now, many theologians disagree on the answer to the following question, but it is an important question. Did God call Israel to do the impossible? No, God did not take Israel through an exercise in futility. Look at Drawing 3.2.

When God called Moses to deliver His people out of Egypt to take them to the land of Canaan, He did not take them out

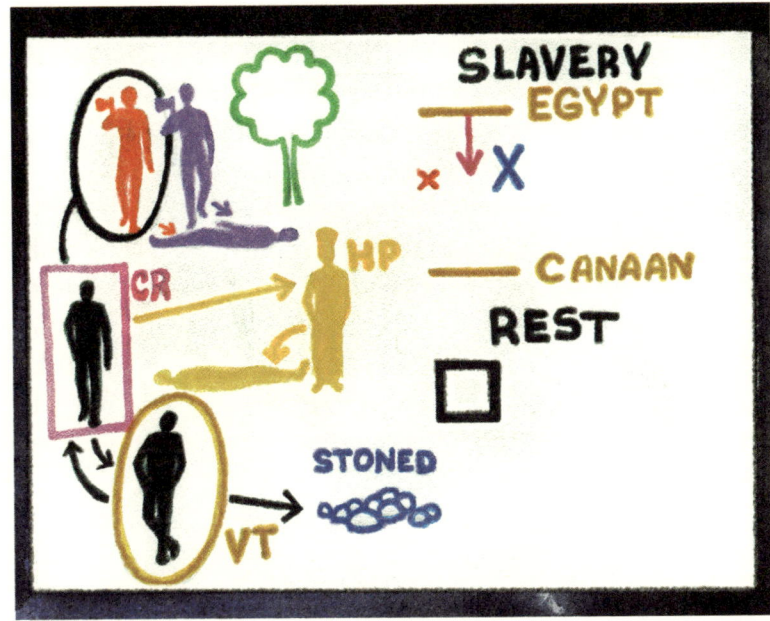

*Drawing 3.2*

into the desert for to kill them. God did not intend to kill them in the desert (big blue x). He fully intended to safely deliver them from slavery to the land of rest.

But at Kadesh Barnea, two years into the trek (small red x), He sent spies in, and ten of the twelve came back and gave a faith-less report after which He said, "Very well, back to the desert you all shall go. I want nothing to do with you anymore. I have had it with this crowd. You shall all drop here in the desert with the exception of Caleb and Joshua, and their families."

The ones to whom the promise and the opportunity were given, failed. In fact, this is the repetitive story of Israel. God renews the covenant with the remnant, starts over, Israel fails. God renews, starts over, Israel fails.

Israel's history proves beyond a shadow of doubt that living by faith is the most difficult experience known to the human race. Today, so few people actually live by faith. A lot of people wear the label as they would wear a watch. A lot of people talk glibly about it but don't have a clue as to what it means experientially. Righteousness by faith is not just a doctrine, it's an experience; and you cannot explain the doctrine until you have lived the experience. You can draw pretty pictures of it, you can voice wonderful platitudes and plaudits about it, but until you live it, you cannot know it. That's the way faith works.

What God was calling Israel to do is only possible by faith. But the carnal heart—and this is where the problem is—cannot live by faith. It is impossible for the carnal heart to live by faith.

Paul says in Romans 8:7, **"The mind governed by the flesh is hostile to God; it does not submit to God's law, nor can it do so."** Those controlled by the sinful nature cannot please God.

Wow! That is hitting the nail on the head.

The reason Israel failed to do what God wanted is because of their sinful, hard, uncircumcised hearts. Israel was to have the privilege of being a kingdom of priests and a holy nation. And this opportunity, this calling, this privilege, has not been seen in the world since. But they failed and God rejected them. Every one of them died in the wilderness except Caleb and Joshua, and their families.

Jump to Revelation 1:5–6. John is writing and has received this prophecy and testimony **"from Jesus Christ, who is the faithful witness, the firstborn from the dead, and the ruler of the kings of the earth. To him who loves us and has freed us from our sins by his blood, and has made us to be a kingdom and priests."**

What John means by **"made us to be a kingdom and priests,"** is explained in Galatians 3:28–29, which says that in Christ, **"There is neither Jew nor Gentile, neither slave nor free, nor is there male and female, for you are all one in Christ Jesus. If you belong to Christ, then..."** guess what? Everything promised to Abraham's offspring, you are and you get! Let me show you another text.

In James 1:1, notice whom James is addressing. He starts by giving his name, "**James, a servant of God and of the Lord Jesus Christ,**" and then he names those to whom the letter is addressing "**to the twelve tribes.**"

My next point is critical.

Do you think James is writing to Abraham's *biological* offspring or to his *spiritual* descendants? "**To the twelve tribes scattered among the nations: Greetings.**"

And to prove that what you just read is true, jump to James 2:1 and notice that he addresses his letter to "**My brothers and sisters, believers in our glorious Lord Jesus Christ.**"

James is writing to the twelve tribes and he recognizes the twelve tribes as being those who believe in Jesus Christ—those who are of the faith of Abraham. This has nothing to do with Abraham's biological offspring.

If you still have a question about this, go to Romans 9:6 and notice what Paul says, "**For not all who are descended from Israel are Israel.**"

This is a problem that is confronting Christianity today and spinning it on its ear. I am not anti-Semitic at all. I am not anti-Catholic. I am not anti-Muslim. I am not anti-anything—except falsehood.

Paul makes it clear, just because your biological father is Abraham, means zero! He says in Romans 9:7, "**Nor because they are his descendants are they all Abraham's children. On the contrary, 'It is through Isaac that your offspring will be reckoned.'**"

Paul shows that it is through the promise, through faith, that the offspring comes. Then in Romans 11, Paul makes it clear that all in Israel who have hard hearts have been cut off of the vine. Its branches have been lopped off and the whole thing has been destroyed.

Understand that to fulfill what God required of Israel, there was only one way to do it. What God requires of you and me, there is only one way to do it—and that's through faith.

Let me give you an example: God may call you to do something on a higher level than you are right now; and the reach on the ladder from where you are, to where He wants you to go, is just a little farther then you can stretch.

When you find yourself here, you only have two choices: 1) Go for it; or 2) Tell God you will only go so far. That's it.

And how much do you think God likes choice number 2? Who becomes sovereign Lord when we say we're only going to do so much and no more?

I encounter a lot of people who tell me, "Larry, it doesn't matter on what day of the week I worship."

I say, "Oh sovereign Lord! You are bigger than God. You have authority over God. If you can tell Him what you will or won't do, that makes you God." If He says, "Do this" and you say, "No, I'm going to do that," that makes you greater than He is.

And if I understand the definition of the word blasphemy, it means to usurp the prerogatives of God.

God has put His children in a world that is contrary to His will for specific reasons. But living by faith in a sinful world is the toughest thing on Earth to do. This is why most people fail miserably at it, although they don't realize the magnitude of their miserable failure. They go on day-by-day, talking the talk, saying the words, but denying the power of God in their religious experience.

In that case, religion becomes a form; it becomes something you do; some external criteria you perform to meet the satisfaction of the social crowd you desire to mingle with.

I'll tell you something about truth, the truth will set you free: free of your friends, free of your family, and ultimately, free of your church!

In the end-time, God does not have a true church—a true denomination—contrary to what the Mormons, the Jehovah's

Witnesses, the Seventh-day Adventists, and other denominations claim. In the end-time, God has a TRUTH and those who love it will cling to it. That's the way it works!

God is going to separate those who love truth by the call and test of faith. The Father is going to put all of the necessities of life into the hands of the devil and his forces. Only those who have the mark of the beast will be able to buy and sell. They're the only ones who will be able to conduct business in exchange for the necessities of life.

And if you cannot live by faith, if you cannot reach beyond what is humanly possible, if you cannot take hold of God's power and do what He wants you to do, then you will have to fall back and accept the mark of the beast.

But for those who live by faith and are cut off entirely from support, one's dependence on God will be all there is. God called Israel to be a kingdom of priests and a holy nation, and that was only possible through faith.

### Shedding of Blood

Now, I want to mention a few more points about the blood covenant because despite the fact I am bringing up a lot of different pieces, I am going to try to bring them together by the end of the chapter.

Notice in Leviticus 17:10 what God says. **"I will set my face against any Israelite or any foreigner residing among them who eats blood, and I will cut them off from the people."** This is why the Jews kill their sacrifices and the animals they eat in a certain way, so that the blood is properly drained from the carcass.

Let me say something about the expression: *cutting off the people*. It is used throughout the Old Testament, time and time again. Being cut off from others is the most dreadful thing that can happen.

In the wilderness, to be put outside the camp meant certain death. Jesus died outside the camp; and the wicked, at the end of the thousand years, will be destroyed outside the camp (Holy City).

Notice why God said He didn't want Israel eating blood. **"For the life of a creature is in the blood, and I have given it to you to make atonement for yourselves on the altar; it is the blood that makes atonement for one's life."**[1]

Why does He say, **"The life of a creature is in the blood?"**

The shedding of blood is actually representing the judicial equilibrium that God requires, life for life. God set up a very neat system in the Old Testament. Let me use an illustration to explain how this works. Look at Drawing 3.2 again.

Let's say two men (red and purple) work together and they go out to chop down trees. You can see that both guys have an axe. But the red man intends to kill the purple man so he can collect his wife or insurance or possessions. So the red aggressor loosens the head of his axe so that, as they're chopping a tree down, the axe head flies off the handle and the purple victim is killed. He's dead. You can see he's lying on the ground.

According to God's economy, the red aggressor is to be killed because life for life is required. You can read about this in Genesis 9, Exodus 21, Numbers 35, Deuteronomy 19, and Proverbs 22.

God requires a life for a life. The law and judicial equilibrium always requires life for life. However, God provided a way for mercy to be extended.

Notice that the red offender is taken to a city of refuge (CR), and in this city, after the elders come together and hear his story, they escort this man to his home village (VT) to stand trial.

After the trial, if it is determined that the red aggressor killed the purple victim INTENTIONALLY, he is immediately led outside the camp and stoned to death. You can picture him under the pile of stones.

---

[1] Leviticus 17:11

Who do you suppose leads in the stoning? The next of kin got the first rock and hurled it at the guilty man. As you can imagine, sometimes justice is a very painful thing to implement and enforce.

Incidentally, in certain cases, when witnesses testified about behavior that was worthy of death, that witness had to lead in the stoning by throwing the first stone.

In other words, if you were going to tattle or complain, you had to be prepared to provide the execution. The responsibility for truth is tremendous and a tough one to bear. Back to Image 3.2.

If in the trial, though, it is found that this man ACCIDENTALLY killed his brother, he goes back to the city of refuge (CR) and lives in the city until the high priest (HP) dies.

What God is showing is that when the high priest dies, the life that is required has been satisfied.

The red man (if he is still living) is free, then, to leave the city of refuge. God transfers the guilt from the guilty to the high priest so that when the high priest dies, the (now) innocent man goes free.

This is why Hebrews 10 says that if we go on sinning after we know the truth, it is no longer accidental, it is deliberate. And no sacrifice (no transference) is possible if the act is deliberate.

However, if we do sin, we do have a high priest who has been slain, and all who are in Christ Jesus are not under condemnation. The life for life concept of judicial equilibrium reverberates all the way from old Eden to new Eden.

What God has been working through over a period of 6,000 years is how to make what was lost, fully restored. And to do this, He took a man called Abraham and said, "Abraham, I need somebody to bear the gospel for me throughout the earth. I need a kingdom of priests. I need a family who understands me, who understands what I am all about, who understands the depths and heights and breadth of my love for mankind, who can understand what salvation's economy and properties are about. And I need some of these people to go throughout the earth to tell the world about me because the world is in ignorance; and even worse, their hearts are hard and they don't want to know me."

When you're born into sin, you are not naturally inclined to want to know about the ways of God. It's too difficult. It's too intrusive. When you come to know God, the first thing you learn is that His will is greater than your will. And to the carnal heart that is the worst thing on Earth to learn. What happens when somebody tells you how you should be doing something? What does the carnal heart do? It rebels. The toughest thing on Earth to do is surrender your will to another.

From Numbers 35:33, I want to point out again that one of the things promised to Abraham is the land. Now, the land is not just a little piece of ground called the Middle East. The whole Earth is the land God has in mind. The whole Earth is what is being discussed. It's truly an incredible story and the particulars are all flushed out in the books of Isaiah, Ezekiel, and Jeremiah. Read those books.

God says, **"Do not pollute the land where you are."** This includes America today. Remember, this is God talking.

**"Bloodshed pollutes the land, and atonement cannot be made for the land on which blood has been shed, except by the blood of the one who shed it."**[1]

Atonement for the land cannot be made except by the one who shed the blood. That is why, when Noah came off the ark, God said, "Listen Noah, whoever kills a man, that murderer is to be put to death—life for life."

Now you can understand why, in Revelation 20, fire comes down from God out of heaven. The Father is Christ's next of kin. This is the reason He is going to slay the wicked at the end of the 1,000 years. The Father will avenge the murder of His

---

[1] Numbers 35:33

Son. All who would have participated in Jesus' murder will be destroyed.

In the first chapter, I made the point, the reason the wages of sin is death by execution is because a sinner would, if he could, set himself up as God. This is what the story of Lucifer and the angels is all about. The story has been preserved to reveal this simple fact.

From Genesis to Revelation there is one grand explanation and theme of how to live by faith and receive the righteousness that comes from God. God said in Numbers 35:34, "**Do not defile the land where you live and where I dwell, for I, the Lord, dwell among the Israelites.**" And in Genesis 9:4 God told Noah, "**But you must not eat meat that has its lifeblood still in it.**"

Now, this is what God told Noah BEFORE there was ever a Jew, or Abraham, or Mount Sinai. This is at the flood. "**And for your lifeblood I will surely demand an accounting. I will demand an accounting from every animal. And from each human being, too, I will demand an accounting for the life of another human being.**"[1] God takes this very seriously.

In Exodus 21:28, if an animal brings about the death of someone and the owner has never seen that animal behave in such a way, that animal is to be put to death. God demands an accounting even from the beasts of the field. The chapter goes on to say that if an ox gores someone to death and the owner knows he has a bad animal because it has hurt others before, the owner is to be put to death with the ox because he is guilty of negligence.

In Genesis 4, Cain asks God, "**Am I my brother's keeper?**" God says to him, "You bet you are. You are your brother's keeper." And then in Genesis 9:6, God affirms this to Noah by saying, "**Whoever sheds human blood, by humans shall their blood be shed; for in the image of God has God made mankind.**"

---

[1] Genesis 9:5

In this section, I am trying to show you the importance of blood, and what a blood covenant really means and implies. Notice what Exodus 21:12–14 says, **"Anyone who strikes a person with a fatal blow is to be put to death. However, if it is not done intentionally, but God lets it happen, they are to flee to a place I will designate. But if anyone schemes and kills someone deliberately, that person is to be taken from my altar and put to death."**

That's the key, if one has motive. This is why, in today's court, we have first-degree, second-degree, and third-degree murder. Motive makes a difference. In other verses, God insists that this be done rapidly—immediately—because in the same verse, He says, "If you allow the penalty to wane or the time to lag, soon, the penalty is lessened and the crime forgotten."

Have you seen any examples of that in the news lately?

Now, some people take the comments of Jesus in Matthew 5 literally, when He said, "You have heard it said from Moses' time, a life for life, eye for eye, tooth for tooth, but I say unto you love your neighbor."

What He was trying to show and emphasize is that, although the law demands life for life, bruise for bruise, eye for eye, and tooth for tooth, judicial equilibrium can be carried to the point of excess. He was remonstrating that there were certain provisions for which mercy could be extended. Remember when they were ready to kill the woman caught in adultery?

In the story, the zealots had picked up rocks and were ready to stone her. They knew there was a provision to extend her mercy but those who had committed adultery with her were not interested in mercy. And yet, Jesus tactfully disarms the whole situation by writing, what I believe, were their names in the sand. God is in the business of saving people, not condemning them. Yes, the Holy Spirit does condemn those who will not surrender. That's the way guilt works. But Jesus came to redeem mankind not to condemn it.

*Unilateral / Bilateral Covenants*

Next, I want to show you two types of covenants and demonstrate them using four examples. Hopefully, in these four examples, you'll be able to see the difference between them and how they operate.

The first example is the covenant God gave to Abraham, which was unilateral. This type is when God said, "I am going to do this. I have chosen you—selected you—because you are a man of faith and I am going to give you this land and make you the father of many nations."[1] Now, Abraham went to his grave without ever seeing it. He died looking forward to it.

Hebrews 11:10 says, Abraham **was looking forward to the city with foundations, whose architect and builder is God.** But what was promised to Abraham hasn't happened yet.

The second example is God's Ten Commandments—the moral law. This is also a unilateral covenant. There is no negotiation on the Ten Commandments. God didn't consult with any human about them. The Ten Commandments are unilateral. Notice the size and scope of this unilateral covenant compared to Abraham's. This type encompasses everyone, everywhere.

The third example is the Levitical system. I use the word Levitical to represent the priesthood of the nation. Choosing the children of Israel to be His kingdom of priests was a bilateral agreement. This means it is conditional. It was made on a blood covenant that God was going to take Abraham's descendants and make them trustees of His gospel. And the only way to be released from a blood covenant is when somebody dies.

Now, don't confuse what God promised Abraham personally (unilaterally) with what He promised Abraham's offspring (bilaterally). Abraham can't make an agreement that binds descendants who haven't been born yet.

This is Lysander Spooner's argument about the U.S. Constitution in his treatise titled *No Treason*. One can't bind following

---

[1] Genesis 15

generations to a contract. No one was saved because Abraham was their father.

Remember, Jesus chastised the Jews in Matthew 3:9 when He said, **"And do not think you can say to yourselves, 'We have Abraham as our father.' I tell you that out of these stones God can raise up children for Abraham."**

The fourth and last example is circumcision. This too was a bilateral covenant. Circumcision was both part of the blood covenant and a sign of the Levitical covenant. So, when Jesus died, circumcision no longer meant anything.

I've listed four examples of two types of covenants, and now would like to walk through each one in more detail.

In Exodus 31:13 the Lord said to Moses, **"Say to the Israelites, 'You must observe my Sabbaths. This will be a sign.'"** Circumcision was a sign of the Levitical covenant. The Sabbath is a sign of the moral covenant.

What is the sign of the covenant for the land mentioned in Genesis 15:5? The stars that represent the group of people no one can count—the people are the sign.

If I said to you, "We'll make an agreement and this pile of rocks will be a witness that we have made this agreement." The pile of rocks would be the sign of the agreement.

When God said to Abraham, "You're childless, but I'm going to promise you a room full of children," the children are the sign. The *sign* of the promise is the *descendants* who come from the child of promise. In the same way, the Sabbath will be a sign.

He then says, **"Observe the Sabbath, because it is holy to you. Anyone who desecrates it is to be put to death; those who do any work on that day must be cut off from their people. The Israelites are to observe the Sabbath, celebrating it for the generations to come as a lasting covenant. It will be a sign between me and the Israelites forever."**[1]

---

[1] Exodus 31:14–17

You can see from this verse there are going to be Israelites forever, because the promise given to Abraham goes all the way to the very end of time. And so the answer to *why a Christian would want to be an heir of Abraham* is because of all that was promised to him. God promised Abraham life eternal and the land. That is everything anyone could possibly need to live for eternity.

*Ten Commandments*

In Deuteronomy 4:13, I want you to see how the Covenant is also the Ten Commandments. Notice how the words are interchangeable. Moses tells the children of Israel that, "**He [God] declared to you his covenant, the Ten Commandments, which he commanded you to follow and then wrote them on two stone tablets.**"

Now, let's take a look at the Levitical system. In Exodus 24:4–7 the Bible says, "**Moses then wrote down everything the Lord had said. He got up early the next morning and built an altar at the foot of the mountain and set up twelve stone pillars representing the twelve tribes of Israel. Then he sent young Israelite men, and they offered burnt offerings and sacrificed young bulls as fellowship offerings to the Lord. Moses took half of the blood and put it in bowls, and the other half he splashed against the altar. Then he took the Book of the Covenant.**"

Understand that the Book of the Covenant is not the two tablets of stone. The Book of the Covenant is what Moses wrote down. We call it the Law of Moses. "**Then he took the Book of the Covenant and read it to the people. They responded, 'We will do everything the Lord has said; we will obey.'**"

They agreed to this not realizing what they were doing. The people had seen the King of the universe shrouded in dark clouds and fiery flames on Mount Sinai, and had been awed into submission; they had seen His magnificence and were afraid. But being awed into submission is no substitute for being transformed by grace. **"Moses then took the blood, sprinkled it on the people and said, 'This is the blood of the covenant that the Lord has made with you in accordance with all these words.'"**[1]

This is a reference to the animals that were laid on the ground and passed through by the Lord in Genesis 15.

**"When the sun had set and darkness had fallen, a smoking firepot with a blazing torch appeared and passed between the pieces. On that day the Lord made a covenant with Abram and said, 'To your descendants I give this land.'"**[2]

What Moses did was take some of that blood—albeit 400 years later—and sprinkled it on the people, because they were willingly entering into the blood covenant just as Abraham had. And once a blood covenant has been agreed upon, no one can get out of the covenant until someone dies.

Notice what Paul says in Hebrews 9:18–22. **"This is why even the first covenant was not put into effect without blood. When Moses had proclaimed every command of the law to all the people, he took the blood of calves, together with water, scarlet wool and branches of hyssop, and sprinkled the scroll** [the little book he had written] **and all the people. He said, 'This is the blood of the covenant, which God has commanded you to keep.'** [We are entering into this bilateral system.] **In the same way, he sprinkled with the blood both the tabernacle and everything used in its ceremonies. In fact, the law requires that nearly everything be cleansed with blood, and without the shedding of blood** [without the giving of life] **there is no forgiveness."** The Levitical system ended when Jesus died. I say this because He told His disciples the night of Passover when He had put the wine into the cup, **"This is my blood of the covenant, which is poured out** [spilled] **for many for the forgiveness of sins."**[3]

---

[1] Exodus 24:8
[2] Genesis 15:17–18
[3] Matthew 26:28

In Genesis 15, God walked through the carcasses; it was His call to die. And when He died, He brought the entire Levitical system to an end. That is what Hebrews 7, Colossians 2, Ephesians 2, and Galatians 3 are all about. All that had been promised, all that had been set up, and all that was put in place was made void.

Look at what Colossians 2:13-15 says. **"When you were dead in your sins and in the uncircumcision of your flesh, God made you alive with Christ. He forgave us all our sins, having canceled the charge of our legal indebtedness, which stood against us and condemned us; he has taken it away, nailing it to the cross. And having disarmed the powers and authorities, he made a public spectacle of them, triumphing over them by the cross"**

Jesus nailed the whole Levitical system to the cross.

The Levitical system required things that are no longer required because Jesus brought the whole system to an end. One of the requirements was tithing. Tithing was nailed to the cross.

As I write this, I know what you're thinking; but notice what Hebrews 7:5 says. **"Now the law requires the descendants of Levi who become priests to collect a tenth from the people."**

Is this talking about the Ten Commandments? Where in the Ten Commandments does it say anything about tithing? It isn't there.

Paul says, **"The law requires the descendants of Levi who become priests to collect a tenth from the people—that is, from their fellow Israelites."**

Jump to Hebrews 7:11, **"If perfection could have been attained through the Levitical priesthood** [the Levitical system]—**and indeed the law given to the people established that priesthood—why was there still need for another priest to come, one in the order of Melchizedek, not in the order of Aaron?** [Now this next part is powerful.] **For when the** priesthood is changed, the law must be changed also." I didn't say that! Paul said it!

Look at Hebrews 7:13–16, "**He of whom these things are said** [speaking of Christ], **belonged to a different tribe, and no one from that tribe has ever served at the altar. For it is clear that our Lord descended from** [the tribe of] **Judah, and in regard to that tribe Moses said nothing about priests. And what we have said is even more clear if another priest like Melchizedek appears, one who has become a priest not on the basis of a regulation as to his ancestry but on the basis of the power an indestructible life.**"

Hebrews 7 teaches that the entire Levitical system was nailed to the cross. That includes tithing. That includes laws regarding clean and unclean food. Take the Levitical system in its entirety and nail it to the cross.

But wait... let me finish my thought. The wisdom of God is revealed in the Levitical system and its laws. And when God writes on your heart (through the Spirit), and grants you understanding of the meaning of these things (through the Spirit), they will find a place in your life. Not on the basis of law, but on the basis of what the Spirit is moving you to do.

I can show you that Abraham tithed before tithing was ever required. I can show you that Jacob did the same. These men tithed because they were led by the Spirit to do so. And those of you who have tithed because you were impressed by the Spirit have been blessed for it. But if you've been tithing to be in accordance with the law, you don't have a clue as to what the experience is really all about.

God intended that tithing be a faith experience, not a standard for righteousness. Everything has been nailed to the cross except two unilateral covenants which cannot be altered. There are only Ten Commandments binding and obligatory upon the human race, no matter where on this planet you live.

However, if you are led of the Spirit, God will lead you (at your own pace) into an experience of faith and you will then discover what the wisdom of God was behind unclean food. And when you begin to see the beauty of it and what it was really all about, you will gladly graft it into your life because of the Spirit's leading, not because it is law.

Righteousness by faith comes as we allow the Spirit to lead us. I guarantee, the Spirit will stretch you beyond what you can reach. He will nag you and work with you until you either rebel or surrender. Those who continue in a course of rebellion will ultimately commit the unpardonable sin.

I'm trying to lay this out in the clearest and simplest of terms, that when one becomes born again, God gives a special gift of the Spirit to guide you into all truth. When you are born again, God gives you special power to reach beyond what you can humanly do. He will take you places you do not want to go. He will show you things you would rather not see. He will test you, He will try you, and He will purge you so that your love for Him and your dependency on Him is complete.

Righteousness by faith is the most beautiful and wonderful doctrine in the whole Bible. But until you've really begun to live it, you cannot possibly understand it. Mental assent cannot and will not work. It is impossible.

When you give your life to Jesus Christ, when you say "Lord, I am willing to go, willing to be, willing to do whatever you call me to do," you have begun the walk of faith, not until.

I had a lot of things to share with you but I've run out of space. However, I can't end this chapter without compelling you to renew your commitment to live by faith, no matter what it cost you—no matter the price. Christ came to redeem you and me, and it is life for life. If you want His righteousness, then you've got to give Him your filth. What a deal! What an offer!

*The whole heart of the
matter is being born again.*

# CHAPTER 4

———

# Overcoming Sin

The Bible describes three types of righteousness, and these three types are classified as two kinds.

Kind 1) GOD (given)
    Type A) Imputed
    Type B) Imparted
Kind 2) HOLINESS (living)
    Type C) Right doing

The first and second *types* of righteousness (*A and B*) come from the same source, God. This is *Kind 1*. Kind 1 is the righteousness that we must have in order to be saved. It's the righteousness that comes by faith. It has nothing to do with the works of man.

The third *type* of righteousness (C) is right doing. This is the basis for holiness, which is *Kind 2*. Kind 2 is a righteousness that is demonstrated by our living. When we do the things God asks us to do, it is a demonstration of holiness; and God calls all of His children to holiness. Paul says without holiness, none of us will see the Lord. But living righteously doesn't mean we have the righteousness of Christ.

The law demands, "thou shalt not kill, thou shalt not commit adultery, thou shalt not covet, etc.," and if we refrain from doing those things, wonderful, but this won't save us. It does not produce the righteousness needed for salvation.

### Imparted / Imputed

The two types, imputed and imparted, make up the kind of righteousness that God Himself provides. For a visual, I like to use the illustration of when Adam and Eve sinned. Jesus killed the lamb and clothed the naked guilty pair symbolizing the gift and covering of His righteousness. What do the words imputed and imparted mean?

Imputed means reckoned to be something even though you really aren't. Imputed is Type A. When we give our lives to Christ and are willing to do all that God asks, we are living by faith. And when we surrender and come to this position in our lives, God imputes the righteousness of Jesus to us.

Type B is imparted, and imparted means you actually possess something—it's yours. A time is coming when the righteousness of Christ will be imparted to us. That means He is going to change the nature of all who live by faith from a sinful nature to a sinless nature. Temptation will no longer be a problem. The slavery of sin will be over, and we will be free from our sinful nature at last. God is going to set His people free.

In Revelation this is called the SEALING.

After looking at the three types of righteousness, let me address how righteousness by faith leads to a holy life, and how its *imitation* leads to *legalism*. I want to describe both sides of the coin because there are two sides.

*Right Doing*

In Romans 3:28, notice what Paul says, **"For we maintain that a person is justified by faith apart from the works of the law."** What this means in plain English is that a person is justified by faith, not works.

Now notice what James 2:24 says, **"You see that a person is considered righteous by what they do and not by faith alone."** Can you see any reason why Martin Luther did not like James?

The two texts seem to contradict each other. For those who are proof text oriented, you can make one text fight against the other; but actually there is a very clear harmony in what is being said when we look beneath the surface and understand the story.

In Romans 1:1–2, Paul identifies himself (as was the custom in those days) and he says, **"Paul, a servant of Christ Jesus, called to be an apostle and set apart for the gospel of God— the gospel he promised beforehand through his prophets in the Holy Scriptures."**

He's saying, "I have been set apart to preach the gospel God promised through his prophets in Scripture." Well, the only Scripture that existed in Paul's day was what we call the Old Testament.

In verse 5, talking about Jesus, he says, **"Through him we received grace and apostleship to call all the Gentiles to the obedience that comes from faith for his name's sake."**

We just read that Paul says a person IS justified by faith alone; but James says that a person IS NOT justified by faith alone. How does all of this come together?

When Jesus lived on Earth, what kind of life did He live?

Look at Drawing 4.1. This is an illustration of the record of Christ's life. This record, written over the thirty-three years of His life, when scrutinized by the law, declared Jesus to be *sinless*. This sinless life is called the righteousness of God.

It is Jesus' righteousness that we must have in order to be

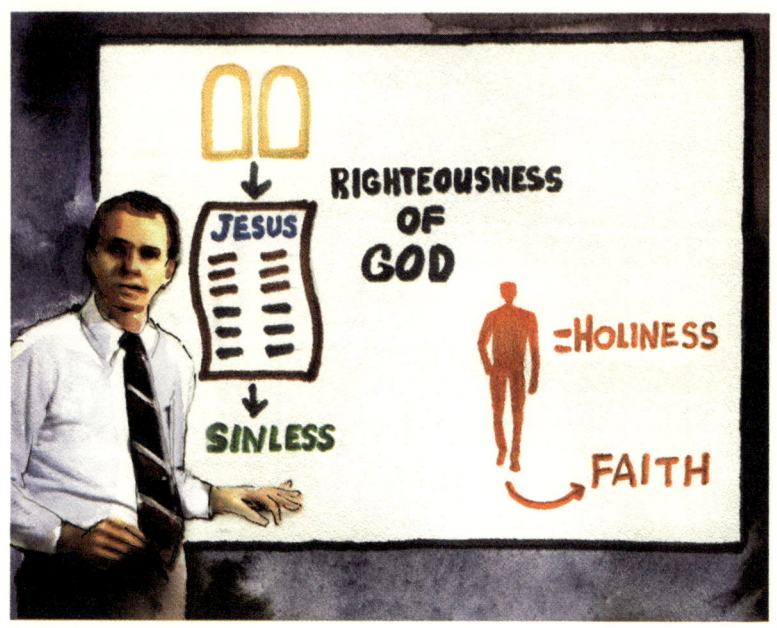

*Drawing 4.1*

saved. We have to somehow acquire this or we can't be justified—EVER. The truth is you and I are sinners and we are
condemned.

Let's read Romans 3:28 again and notice what Paul is saying, **"For we maintain that a person is justified by faith apart
from the works of the law."**

Hold that thought in your mind and look at what Romans
1:17 says, **"For in the gospel the righteousness of God is
revealed."**

Next, look at Romans 3:21 and notice what is said there,
**"But now apart from the law the righteousness of God has
been made known."** Paul is referring to the life of Christ.

Now, consider what Romans 5:10 says. **"For if, while we
were God's enemies, we were reconciled to him through the
death of his Son, how much more, having been reconciled,
shall we be saved through his life!"** Paul is saying that if we
do the things required of the gospel as the Spirit convicts us,

this produces *holiness*. And the evidence of holiness reveals our *faith*.

In other words, if I say to you, "For me, it is a conscientious matter that I should do this or I should not do this," I am expressing my faith in what I believe the Holy Spirit would have me do. But my faith and the holiness that is being expressed won't save me.

Let me try and explain the way this works.

God looks over me and says, "Well good, Larry is living by faith. Let's take the righteousness of Christ and put it over Larry's life." So the end result is, when God looks at me, He sees the perfect life of Christ covering my sinful life and I am, at that moment, justified by the righteousness of Christ—not by my own doing. This takes a righteousness that comes from God, a righteousness that is apart from law, and I can only get that righteousness through faith.

James 2:21-24 says, **"Was not our ancestor Abraham considered righteous for what he did when he offered his son Isaac on the altar? You see that a person is considered righteous by what they do and not by faith alone."**

I need to elaborate on Abraham's story a bit more.

God called Abraham to do the most difficult thing a human being has ever been called to do. Even more difficult than giving up your own life would be to take the life of your child.

I know something about the love a father has for his daughter. If God called me and said "Take your child and go to the nearest mountain and offer her up as a sacrifice," I would not be able to do that.

What Abraham was called to do was the supreme sacrifice. God wanted one person on Earth to understand what He would have to experience to save the world.

And so, faithful Abraham gets Isaac out of bed, they load up the donkey, they get the firewood and everything else they need, and they go. And as they're walking along to Mount

Moriah, young Isaac looks around and says, "Dad, where's the sacrifice?"

Abraham simply says, "It will be provided." And they keep walking until, finally they're on top of the mountain.

Well, after they've built the altar, Abraham sits down on a rock, he looks at Isaac and says, "Son, you are the sacrifice."

Could you do that to your child? And as Abraham raised the knife, God called out "Abraham, Abraham, I have seen your faith."

Abraham believed because he knew that God would raise Isaac up if necessary to fulfill the promise He had made. How many people could do such a thing?

What James is trying to explain in James 2:21–24 is that when God sent Abraham the message, Abraham believed God and went forward to do what he was called to do. Abraham demonstrated his faith by what he did.

**"And the scripture was fulfilled that says, 'Abraham believed God, and it was credited to him as righteousness,' and he was called God's friend. You see that a person is considered righteous by what they do and not by faith alone."**

*Legalism / Faith*

I would like for you to consider what legalism and faith are, and what the difference is between the two. In Drawing 4.2 is a man who is a sinner out in the world, having no knowledge of God, having no spiritual life at all. One day, the Holy Spirit comes to this man and brings a spiritual awakening to his heart.

Through the years, I have found there is a consistent way to identify a spiritual awakening. I call it a nagging—a spiritual nagging. It's something that is going on inside and won't let you rest. The Holy Spirit brings guilt and this nagging is the response to the guilt.

Guilt, inherently, is not bad. God designed us so that we can

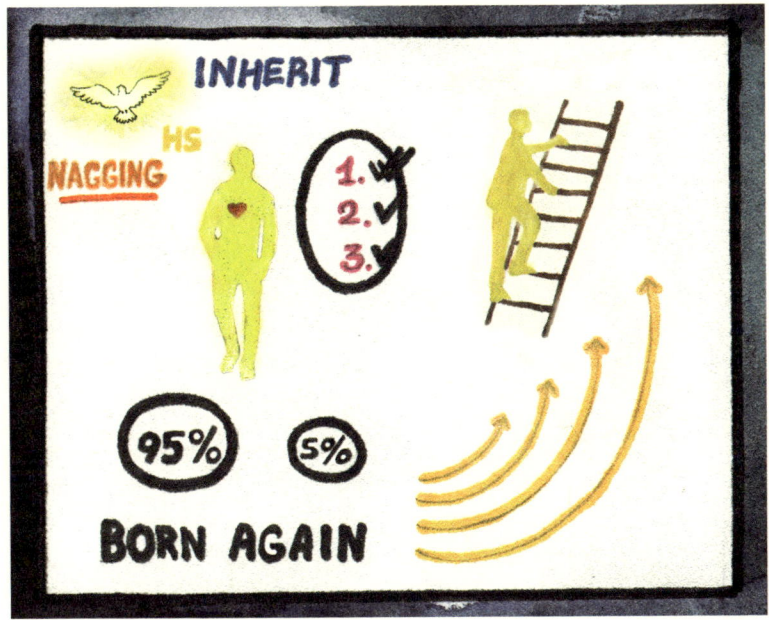

*Drawing 4.2*

sense it and when it's present, the nagging motivates us to get rid of it.

Guilt is to the spiritual appetite what hunger is to our stomach. Guilt will take your sleep from you. It will take your happiness from you. It can even take your life from you, if not dealt with properly.

When a person becomes born again, the Holy Spirit comes and begins working on the heart by bringing a relentless nagging (guilt), and the nagging is always about doing something we really would prefer not to do.

What He's trying to do is wrestle with us until we have surrendered all. He wants us to surrender our will, to do what God requires, and forget the consequences. The consequences will be the means by which the glory of God is revealed through us to others.

But if we focus on the consequences, we get into this back-and-forth loop that we can't get out of. And this see-saw effect is what James is talking about when he describes a person that is unstable, wavering about, tossed to and fro.

When we open our heart to the Holy Spirit, we have to accept the fact that we are going to ignore the consequences and go forward as God has called us. When we do, the most wonderful thing will overtake us—it's called peace. And where we once had forty friends, we may only have four left, but we'll have peace. Better to have four friends than forty and still have the nagging.

Eventually though, if we refuse the Holy Spirit and put Him off, He will finally leave us and say, "Very well, I'll leave you to your own desires." This is called the unpardonable sin.

When I gave my heart to the Lord, I said, "Lord, I am willing to go and be and do whatever you want." And I had peace in my heart for about thirty minutes. My wife said, "Larry, I think the Lord is calling you to the ministry."

I said, "Oh no. The last thing on Earth I want to do is be a preacher." All the preachers I had known were duds. I didn't really have much respect for preachers, so I didn't want to perpetuate the persona.

But the Lord doesn't give up, and He finally persuaded me that I should be a preacher. He didn't have to knock me off the donkey, but it was close. And that which I dreaded the most, I now love the best. That's the way God works! He knew what He had put within me and how He had equipped me. He knew that, only in doing what He had equipped me to do, would I really be happy. And I can think of nothing else that makes me happier than sharing the gospel. It has brought me more friends than I could have had otherwise.

So the Holy Spirit comes in, brings guilt (nagging), and when we surrender, we receive peace. This is a daily process, because God is ever trying to get us to move up to a higher standard of experience for our lives. Drawing 4.2 illustrates this climb.

God's ideal for us is higher than we can conceptualize. He has a better plan for our lives than we can dream. When we allow the Spirit to lead us, we are able to accomplish more than we ever could have otherwise.

And sometimes, we will experience that the rungs on the ladder are too far apart, so we'll have to let go of one to reach the next. And the scary part is—we might not make it. But the ladder of faith is ever onward and upward. It never ends.

This is how we grow in grace and are sanctified through faith. It is God's great joy to reveal Himself through each of His children in a unique way. God does not give everyone the same talents. He has given all of us special gifts though, and as we allow Him to work in our lives, He develops us into all that He wants us to be.

### Legalism is Works Based

Let me show you where legalism comes into play. Look at Drawing 4.2 again. Here's the same guy going about his day, and the Holy Spirit comes and brings a nagging. This person begins enumerating all the things that qualify him to be holy, and says, "I go to church (1). I behave like everybody else around me (2). I sing in the choir and serve on the board (3). I do all these wonderful things (extra check on 1). I've checked all the right boxes. Leave me alone!" This person has a form of godliness but denies the power necessary to climb the ladder.

Growing up in a Christian home is, in some ways, more difficult to the process of becoming born again than coming from a non-Christian home—because children inherit the patterns and culture of their parents.

If the parents go to church on Wednesday, their children will go to church on Wednesday. 95 percent of the world's population will not change religion. Only 5 percent make the change. This statistic reveals the hold religion has on people.

If you are born a Catholic, chances are 95 percent that you will die a Catholic. If you are born a Mormon, chances are 99 percent! The nature of religion is powerful and has a tenacious grip on the human family. God knows that.

As I write this in 2020, the world has around 1.9 billion Muslims. What is the likelihood of a Muslim becoming a Jew? Zero. What is the likelihood of a Jew becoming a Muslim? Less than zero! Everybody has his own religion, and to get out of its hold is practically impossible.

I have wondered many times how God is going to get the gospel message to everybody everywhere so that truth can save all who are willing to be saved.

Don't misunderstand my previous statement about the downside of being born into a religious home. Being born into religion has some good points, but it's not optimal because children grow up and inherit God. It is inevitable.

The trouble is, God has no grandchildren. Everyone is born again as a child of God; and the born-again experience is unique to each person. The question is, will we open our hearts and let the Holy Spirit have control. That's what matters.

Now, legalism acts very differently. When a legalistic person inherits religion, he knows all the right things to do and all the right things to say. He goes to church at the appointed time. He goes through the rituals of religion. He looks like a Christian, therefore, he must be a Christian. Well, not so. A person like this is a legalist.

In Drawing 4.3, notice the ladder I mentioned earlier. Along comes some truth. Along comes a deeper understanding of God's Word. And when it makes contact with this legalistic person, it's rejected because it's different than what they've been taught. I have heard the expression, "I wasn't taught that" hundreds of times, as though someone else is responsible for their knowledge of Christ, and they're just required to learn the material to pass the quiz.

John 16:13 says, **"But when he, the Spirit of truth, comes, he will guide you into all the truth."** The Holy Spirit teaches

*Drawing 4.3*

everyone the same thing about truth; maybe not at the same time, but it is still the same truth.

Legalism is all about establishing our righteousness by right doing. And I must confess that for many years I was a legalist. Not intentionally; I didn't even know it. I was blind and naked and in need, and didn't know it. Then one day, the Holy Spirit came to me and said, "Larry, you're doing all the right things, but that will not produce the salvation you need because you still don't have the righteousness of Christ. Without His righteousness your chances are zero. If Jesus righteousness is not given to you, I don't care how many good deeds you do, they will not help you get to heaven."

I said, "Oh Lord, what are we going to do?"

He said, "Well, the first thing I'm going to do is help you learn to live by faith. I am going to give you some new understandings and this is going to challenge your faith, and you'll be tested time and time again about what you've learned."

Then, the Lord led me into a wonderful study of His Word that changed my whole life. He rearranged my understanding of salvation and how it works. He revealed the final end-time story and clarified all that Jesus is. And sure enough, my life has changed! I remember one night thinking about the consequences of what the Lord was calling me to do—to give up my job, my career. To just walk away is a pretty heavy call. And because I was in the religion business already, I knew that, in walking away, it was a one-way street—there was no going back. I also knew that in taking a definite stand on certain issues, I would lose my reputation. Legalists are very concerned about their reputations.

I had always held, since becoming a Christian, that serving the Lord was the greatest and most wonderful thing I could do, and I wanted to do that. I was sincere in heart. But I also knew that in following the Spirit, if I took this step, I could fall flat on my face and end up having to get a job that I didn't like for the rest of my life. Yet, when God calls, you have to let the consequences fall by the wayside. When that nagging is present and persistent, and deep down you know it is God speaking to you, like Abraham, you have do something about it. A person is justified by what he does and not by faith alone. We show our faith by our actions. We show what we believe by doing. Not to merit salvation; God grants the salvation because of our demonstration of faith. Do you realize what this really does to our whole understanding?

*1) It means, I really cannot judge anyone.*

You may have a conviction brought by the Holy Spirit in your heart. How can I say that the Spirit is, or isn't, influencing you? This is why Scripture says, "Judge no man; God will judge."

*2) When the Holy Spirit comes in and takes over and you go through the born-again experience, the consequences are immaterial.*

You have one thing in mind and that is to glorify God. Sometimes this will be a tough challenge. Sometimes it will take everything within you; but the harder the test, the greater the glory for God.

Down through the centuries, the way martyrs could stand firm in their faith while being burned at the stake, is they could glorify God in their dying for Him. They understood that when we become Christian we are only careful about one thing, and that is representing the character of God to the best of our ability.

The greatest deception is to take a person who is really a legalist and have him think he is living by faith. The devil is a master at this. The legalist does not hear the Spirit; he looks at the rules. The guiding beacon for the legalist is what was done before, what are the patterns, what will fly best, what is expedient, what is socially acceptable.

A legalist is usually very sociable and enjoys the social aspects of religion, and any disruption of their social standing and social stature is a real problem.

The legalist is not moved by the Spirit. If the Spirit called you to do something strange that would set you free of all your friends and your church membership, would you be prepared to do it?

When we follow the Spirit, we have that kind of surrender constantly on the table. When we live by faith and follow the Spirit, we go where the Spirit leads and let the circumstances fall by the wayside. Those who live by faith are constantly asking God, "What would you have me do? Show me, reveal to me, your will. Show me how I can glorify you in what I am doing today. Help me to see that my first work is to glorify you." This is what living by faith is all about.

The Spirit will take you places you never thought you wanted to go. I guarantee it. The Spirit will lead you to do things you never wanted to do. I guarantee it. But the Spirit will bring

*Drawing 4.4*

you joy you never thought possible. I guarantee it!

In Hebrews 12:4–6 Paul says, **"In your struggle against sin, you have not yet resisted to the point of shedding your blood. And have you completely forgotten this word of encouragement that addresses you as a father addresses his son? It says, 'My son, do not make light of the Lord's discipline, and do not lose heart when he rebukes you, because the Lord disciplines the one he loves, and he chastens everyone he accepts as his son.'"** Have you been spanked by the Lord lately?

*Discipline and Punishment*

Look at Drawing 4.4 and see if this makes sense. When the Holy Spirit comes to us, He speaks to the heart. The heart is where we feel things. On the other hand, the Word (Scripture) speaks to the brain. The brain is where we understand and reason things; where we create models to compare with new things we learn and experience. This is why Scripture says the greatest of all the commandments is to "Love the Lord thy God with all thy heart, mind, and [together they make] the soul."[1]

The previous verse in Hebrews said, "The Lord punishes everyone He accepts as a son." This means the Holy Spirit should be working on your heart right now about something in your life that needs improving, changing, modifying.

The Holy Spirit should be prompting you (nagging you) about something right now, because somewhere in your life "something" needs improving.

Do you hear anything? Are you listening for the Spirit's voice? Or, have you crowded so much stuff into your heart and head that His voice is muted? If we aren't careful, we can cram so much into life that the Spirit is totally drowned out. It's the guilt that propels us to resolve the nagging and have peace.

And that peace will come. It comes for a while until the Holy Spirit brings guilt about the next "something" He wants us to correct. Then the process starts again.

*Limitation of Willpower*

In the late 60's, I was drafted into the Army, and to this day I can remember all the curse words I ever heard. I understand from friends that the cursing was even worse in the Navy! For some reason, once you hear all those words, they never leave your mind. They stay there. The trick though is not to use them, especially when things get out of hand.

I have found only one way to gain victory over things that beset us. I have tried two ways, but have found one that works. The way that *does not* work, I guarantee it, is willpower. The human will is wonderful and it can do much, but it cannot make the carnal heart pure. "The leopard cannot change his spots, the Ethiopian cannot change his skin, and neither can you, who are accustomed to doing evil, do good."

I just paraphrased Jeremiah 13:23.

You cannot make yourself pure. It is impossible no matter how hard you try. The Bible says, "The pure in heart will see

---

[1] Matthew 22:37

God."[1] This implies God will settle for nothing less than a pure heart. Yes, willpower has its place, willpower has its function, but willpower cannot make you, give you, produce within you, a pure heart.

Now, some people come from the womb predisposed to be more righteous than others. They don't seem to have all the bad habits; they don't have all the problems; they don't have all the monkeys on their backs. Some people naturally just seem to be more righteous.

The truth is, we are all carnal and damaged from birth. We come from the womb that way. But God wants purity, so what are we to do? I need to tell you a story—a personal testimony. It's not very pretty but it will make the point.

### The Billboard

In 1973, I was giving Bible studies in Texas. At the same time, Mexicana airline was having a big promotion advertising low fares to Acapulco. And on one of the main highways that run through Dallas, they had a billboard that was ninety feet wide. A normal billboard is sixty feet wide, but this was ninety—it was huge! And to make their ads attractive they had on this sign, a naked woman lying on her side. I think she wore three lilies. That was it. It was truly the most amazing poster I had ever seen!

I had to drive by this sign because we lived in the south part of town, and the only way to get to the north part of town was this expressway. Here I was, driving to a Bible study thinking about this billboard. I tried all sorts of things to keep from looking at this giant naked woman. I would drive by in the left lane looking at the speedometer. Several times I almost wrecked my car trying to look anywhere but in her direction.

The devil will stop at nothing to entice us into sin. But what can we do about sin's attraction? How can one avoid temptation?

---

[1] Matthew 5:8

I remember thinking to myself, I know God is not pleased when we dwell and focus on sexual immorality—because that's basically what the advertisement was all about. There is something about a naked woman that dilates the eyes of men. How many men reading this will admit that?

*(Yeah, and the rest of you are liars!)*

Studies have been done repeatedly and confirm that placing naked women before the eyes of men will cause the pupils to dilate. There is a physiological response. The devil knows it. Believe me, he knows it. And he's working from every angle to destroy mankind.

When I look back on that experience, I'm glad it was placed there, because it taught me the first lesson I needed to know about overcoming sin. That is, unless the victory is accomplished through the Spirit, it is neither permanent nor long-lasting. The whole problem stemmed from my carnal nature. And in realizing this, I was forced to admit that willpower could not change me.

I began to pray, "Lord, you've got to change my nature because that's where the problem rests. You have to help me see this for what it really is, rather than just a moment of pleasure. Help me to see sin for what it really is." Then, by the power of the Spirit, not by the power of Larry, I came to where I had no interest in looking at that billboard. It was the Spirit that changed something within me.

Now, I'm not saying that the Holy Spirit changed everything at once. This was just one test. But I learned a valuable lesson. The Holy Spirit was nagging me about this whole process, because what God wanted to reveal in me was His power to do the impossible. This doesn't make me righteous, I'm still a sinner. But it does teach me something about what God wants to do within me. And when faced with temptation—when struggling with temptation—the only way to overcome it is through the power of the Spirit. If you wrestle with God on your knees and ask Him, "Lord, take this desire from me, I know it's wrong. Take this from me, I can't take it from myself." Faith is where victory begins.

1 John 1:9 says, **"If we confess our sins, he is faithful and just and will forgive us our sins and purify us from all unrighteousness."**

Through this experience, I discovered the critical point: Until I am willing to admit something is sin, I really have no assurance of the power to overcome it. We have to be willing to say to ourselves, THIS IS SIN.

When the Holy Spirit starts nagging and that guilt starts coming, we will resolve it pretty quickly. We'll either put it on the back burner and go on to other things, or we'll resolve it like the Spirit wants. This is the way human nature works. Let me give you an example.

The Tenth Commandment says, "Thou shalt not covet." What does the word 'covet' mean? To want or desire something which belongs to someone else.

Advertising is built around the idea that you can induce people to want something they don't have. If advertisers can present something in the right light, they can induce someone to desire a product. This is why advertisers spend billions of dollars; it's why catalogs are mailed in such great quantities. They're trying to make you want something. They want your money and need you to want their product. That is what advertising is all about.

We live in a world that is designed to produce dissatisfaction. No one has contentment with what they have. What we already have is never enough. Everybody wants more.

Paul says in 1 Timothy 6:6 that, **"Godliness with contentment is great gain."** Are you content with what God has given you? Are you happy with what you have? Are you really pleased with what God has bestowed upon you, or are you driven for more?

Now, I'm not referring to excellence in our work, or endeavoring to advance our responsibilities. I'm talking about the appetite of the heart.

Zig Ziegler once said, "God will give you all the money you can possibly manage. If you don't believe it, notice how much you have." Look at what He has given you. Are you managing your assets, are you managing your time, are you managing your little world to the glory of God?

The Bible says, "To him that knoweth to do BAD and doeth it anyway, to him it is sin." Oops... No, it doesn't say that! It says, **"To him that knoweth to do GOOD and doeth it NOT, to him it is sin."**[1] This verse confirms there is the sin of commission and the sin of omission—both kinds.

When we come face-to-face with sin, there is only one way out, and that's on our knees asking God for the power to overcome. Seven times in the book of Revelation, Scripture uses the term, "To him that overcometh."

Now, what God calls you to overcome may be different than what He requires of me. Your tests and trials should be different because our lives and circumstances are different, but the same general principles are at work.

One of the biggest areas for struggling with willpower is in New Year's resolutions. Have you seen one yet that worked? Sure, we can refrain for 30 days, but then, that's the end of that. It doesn't work because people will not confess sin so they can go to the Spirit and get the power to overcome it.

All around the world, there are people in every nation, kindred, and tongue who live according to the Spirit; who follow the leading of the Spirit; who know the Spirit's nagging in their life; who listen and respond to the Spirit's call. Some are Muslim, some are Jewish, some are Catholic, some are Protestant, some are Hindus, and some are even Pagan.

All over this world, there are people who follow the Spirit,

---

[1] James 4:17

because the Spirit speaks to all of us. In Joel 2:28, the Bible says, in the last days God is going to pour out His Spirit on all people; and that means everybody, everywhere! The Holy Spirit is going to be giving the gospel proclamation throughout the world, working through the 144,000.

*The Sabbath*

The Sabbath is so important to God that He is going to see it is proclaimed to every nation, every language, and every population. Its importance revolves around it being a sign of God's unilateral covenant with mankind. During the Great Tribulation, circumstances are going to be set up so the only way we will be able to keep the Sabbath is through faith.

Consider the 1.4 billion people in China for a moment. When the gospel is preached there, those who live by faith and know the power and working of the Spirit are going to receive the truth about the Sabbath, rejoice, and implement it in their lives. Those in India, those in Russia, those in America will do the same.

God is going to demonstrate to the universe that His salvation will save anyone who lives by faith! People who have open hearts to hear what the Spirit says and have cultivated listening to Him are going to be amazed at what is produced when He floods the world with Truth, and the Sabbath is proclaimed. The result will be a harvest that is numberless.

A multitude that cannot be numbered will come out of the Great Tribulation. What this demonstrates is that God has people in every language, every religion, and every nation who listen to the Spirit.

Now, they may not understand everything quite like you or me, but God doesn't require that. Salvation comes by faith. And when we live up to all that the Spirit leads us to do, God says, "That is a demonstration of faith and I save people on the basis of faith; and because I consider that person saved, give him the righteousness of Christ."

This is how, when we get to heaven, we will not all be in agreement about religion. It's going to take a while to work things out with a Muslim and a Hindu and a Baptist.

Revelation 22:1–2 says, **"Then the angel showed me the river of the water of life, as clear as crystal,** [no water purifier needed] **flowing from the throne of God and of the Lamb down the middle of the great street of the city. On each side of the river stood the tree of life, bearing twelve crops of fruit, yielding its fruit every month. And the leaves of the tree are for the healing of the nations."**

This means God's children are going to gather once a month around the tree of life and get acquainted with Jesus and each other. And in the shade of the tree of life, the great dispersion of the nations of the world into languages and cultures and groups, will all be reunited and brought back into one loving family. Beneath the tree of life, the leaves will produce the shade under which we will sit and learn of God's love and salvation. And what is now a very diverse family will, once again, be like-minded and cohesive.

Abraham was promised he would be the father of many nations. And for a while, when we get there, there will be many nations. But ultimately, "There will be a healing of all the nations, and there will be one Lord, one faith, and one body."[1]

We are about to enter a new age. It will be a very short time period in which the Holy Spirit will be poured out upon all flesh. From it, there will be a great harvest of innumerable people who have been victorious over the beast.

In Revelation 15:1–3, John says, **"I saw in heaven another great and marvelous sign: seven angels with the seven last plagues—last, because with them God's wrath is completed. And I saw what looked like a sea of glass glowing with fire and, standing beside the sea, those who had been victorious over the beast and its image and over the number of its name. They held harps given them by God and sang the song of**

---

[1] Revelation 22:2

God's servant Moses and of the Lamb: 'Great and marvelous are your deeds, Lord God Almighty. Just and true are your ways, King of the nations.'"

This group of people standing there has been victorious over the image. That tells us they live during the Great Tribulation, and they're singing a song of praise.

In chapter two I asked, "Why would any Christian want to be an heir of Abraham?" Isaiah 60:21–22 has the answer.

God says the time is coming when **"All your people will be righteous and they will possess the land forever. They are the shoot I have planted, the work of my hands, for the display of my splendor. The least of you will become a thousand, the smallest a mighty nation. I am the Lord; in its time I will do this swiftly."**

The day is coming when all of God's people, through the power of the Spirit, will be declared righteous. Jesus says, "The time is coming when I am going to write my laws in their hearts and minds. I am going to make this a new covenant with them. No longer will one man say to another, 'know the Lord!' For you will all know me."[1]

We read earlier in Hebrews that a time is coming when God is going to impart a new nature. The struggle with sin will finally be over. We read in Revelation that those who maintain their faith and gain the victory over the beast and his image will face the most strenuous test ever put before mankind. This is why I wanted to write about righteousness by faith; for if we can learn to live by faith now, we will be prepared to stand then.

There is a phenomenon when you're in a boat going down a river. The end is always right in front of you until you get there, and then the end of the river has moved to the next turn. Then, when you get to that next turn, oops, now the river goes another way. Walking by faith is like going down the river. The

---

[1] Hebrews 8:10–11

end is always in sight until you get there, and then it moves.

Abraham looked up at the stars that night and God said, "Count them if you can Abraham because that is the number of your offspring."[1] The Bible says, **"Abraham believed God, and it was credited to him as righteousness,"** and at this time Abraham didn't even have one child yet. What an amazing demonstration of faith.[2]

Dear friends, if you will take hold of God's hand—if you will take hold of what He offers through the Spirit, and let Jesus do for you what you cannot do for yourself—you will have peace through your faith.

And best of all, you will receive the righteousness of Christ which is promised to all who live by faith. Then, every night when you go to sleep, you can have the full assurance of God's salvation.

I go to sleep every night thanking God for something I do not have—salvation. I don't have it. You can search my pockets, my car, my house—it's not there. I do not have salvation. I have the *assurance* of salvation, and with God that's just as good as the real thing. I go to bed every night thanking God for His assurance, and you can too.

Pray with me.

Oh Father in heaven, we understand more of your wonderful ways and the offer of Jesus. He says come unto Him and He will give us rest. We're so glad, so thankful, that Jesus is willing to serve as our Intercessor; He is willing to give us His righteous life; He is willing to redeem us and to save us, if only we are willing to live by faith. Oh God, make us willing. Help us to surrender all. Help us to walk with you as Noah, Enoch, Abraham, and others.

Lord, give us the courage to do what is impossible. Give us the strength to stand against the enmity and hostility of the world. Give us the power of love that we might share and

---

[1] Genesis 15:5
[2] James 2:23

tell others what a wonderful God you are. Thank you for the privilege of knowing you. Now keep us and watch over us is our prayer, in Jesus' name, amen.

# CHAPTER 5

# Two Types of Covenants

In this chapter, I want to clarify and expand upon the blood covenant and, hopefully, simplify it at the same time.

In Genesis 12, 13, and 14, God made a unilateral covenant with Abraham. God promised Abraham the land and that he would be the father of many nations. Because it was God who made the promise, it will certainly happen.

Then, in Genesis 15, God entered into a bilateral covenant with the descendants of Abraham who did not yet exist. In fact, Abraham was still childless when the promise was made.

Think about what God was doing. He was entering into a covenant with people who did not yet exist, through a man who had no children! It makes no sense. But God doesn't see things the way they are, God sees things for what they could be.

In Genesis 15:2, Abraham was concerned about what was promised and asked the Lord, **"What can you give me since I remain childless?"**

What Abraham was really asking is, "How will I know that what you have promised will come true?" So, God took him outside, had him look up at the stars, and said, "Abraham, if you can count the stars, you'll be able to count your offspring."

The Bible says, "Abraham believed God and God credited it to him as righteousness."[1] This means Abraham went away from that meeting with perfect peace that, somehow, in God's good time, this would all come about. When you take God at His Word and believe in His ability to do anything, you should be able to walk away in peace.

Now, Abraham lost that peace a few years later when he and Hagar and Sarah worked out a plan to fulfill God's promise. Their impatience got the better of them and you know what a mess that turned out to be. The Middle East is still reeling from the consequence of their infidelity.

In Genesis 17:18, we see the Lord would not honor Ishmael as the firstborn. Abraham said, "O Lord, won't you pass this [bilateral covenant] on to Ishmael?" And the Lord said, "No, I won't. Ishmael will become the father of a great nation; but no, the covenant will not be done through him."

The Lord then said to Abraham, "Go get five animals. We're going to make this bilateral covenant a blood covenant." And the only way out of this covenant will be the death of the one who initiates it.

God initiated this covenant. In fact, He called this covenant "My Covenant" nine times in Genesis 17.

The five animals Abraham gathered were: a heifer, a ram, a goat, a pigeon, and a dove. The larger animals Abraham cut in two; the birds were not.

Now, Abraham went into a deep sleep, and the Bible tells us that "God came and spoke to him, and Abraham saw a smoking pot and a blazing torch walk through the parts."

Jesus was the individual that walked through the parts,

---

[1] Romans 4:3

although He wasn't called Jesus at the time. He didn't take that name until He was born of Mary; but He's the same member of the Godhead. Jesus walked through the blood and made this covenant with Abraham on behalf of his descendants.

At this point, God had already made a unilateral covenant with Abraham. What God was doing was setting up a bilateral covenant with Abraham's descendants.

The reason this was a two-sided covenant was that, if one party wanted out, the covenant could be broken. Even more significantly, the only way this covenant could be canceled was for God, the one who actually ratified it, to die. So, the animals were slain, Jesus passed through the bodies, and Abraham's descendants had a blood covenant.

Understand, the covenant God offered to the offspring of Abraham 430 years after the Exodus (at Mt. Sinai), was not new nor unique. It was, instead, a repetition and enlargement of what had been extended to the human race through Adam and Eve.

Now, the bilateral covenant offered at Mt. Sinai included new features such as the privilege of being a kingdom of priests, but it remained a conditional two-sided covenant. "If you will be my people, then I will be your God."[1]

This is why Moses told the people, just a few days before God came down on Mount Sinai, that God was coming to renew the blood covenant.

In Deuteronomy 7:6, Moses said, "God has chosen you to be a holy nation, a kingdom of priests." The function of a priest is to serve God and man, and God wanted a nation of baby Abrahams to serve Him.

After God gave Moses the *Laws of Moses*, Moses came down off the mountain, wrote them in a book, and gathered all the people together. Exodus 24:7 says, then, "Moses read the entire book to them." After which, Moses slaughtered an animal,

---

[1] Leviticus 26; Deuteronomy 28–30

dipped a hyssop branch into the bowl of blood, sprinkled the people, and they entered into the blood covenant.[1] Thus, the blood covenant was renewed with the descendants of Abraham.

Why did God choose the same five animals used in the sanctuary service? He did so because some of the descendants of Abraham would be poor and some rich. The poorest offering was a dove. The most expensive, which was offered by the high priest on the Day of Atonement, was a heifer.

God was including every one of Abraham's descendants in this covenant, regardless of social stature. This is why James says that we should not distinguish between the rich and poor in our fellowship, for in God's sight, we are all equal. He loves us all the same.

Now, let me explain something about this blood covenant.

Notice that Drawing 5.1 has a timeline with Calvary indicated by a cross. When the blood covenant was set up with Abraham, God initiated it by passing through the carcasses. This blood covenant was renewed and put into effect at Sinai (Blue X). God finally got the children of Israel into the Promised Land (PL) and He wanted to make them a light unto the world.

In Acts 13:47, Paul clearly understood this, and said that, "God chose Israel to be a light to the world so they could bring the message of salvation to the Gentiles." But on the way to fulfilling God's will, their hard hearts prevented them from accomplishing all that God wanted.

Israel has a 1,400 year history, from the Exodus to the time of Calvary, and one word sums it up—Apostasy. This was Israel's experience time after time. It's the experience of the human race.

### Carnal at Birth

When parents decide to have children, they start with good intentions. But the two parents, who are born again and love

---

[1] Exodus 24:8

*Drawing 5.1*

the Lord with all their hearts—no matter how hard they try—give birth to a carnal baby (NB).

I have never seen two born-again parents give birth to a born-again baby. It never happens. The little rascal is as mean as he can be. He comes out that way! And if you don't curb his will quickly, by the time he's nine years old, he'll think he's God, ordering everybody around and telling them what to do and how to do it. And if you cross him, he'll throw a tantrum that would embarrass anybody. I've seen it in the grocery store. No two born-again parents have ever produced a born-again baby.

Now, here's where legalism takes over. The born-again parents are happy in their love for Jesus and have a happy home. But, lo and behold, junior doesn't share their vision.

Yes, he's taken to church every week. Yes, he's taught what is right and wrong. Yes, he's told all of the good stuff he should do and bad stuff he shouldn't, but his little carnal heart is as hard as a brick. And this little baby can become a 40-year old adult doing all the right things, yet have a heart that's still made of concrete.

What I have just described is a legalist. A legalist is convinced that if he's doing everything right, then God has nothing to hold against him.

I was once giving a seminar and during my presentation I said, "Everyone here who isn't born again is hostile to God." There was a man sitting on the front row, who obviously took offense to my statement, and said, "I'm not hostile toward God. I've got nothing against Him."

I looked at him—he was a swell guy, I'm sure—and I said to him, "You don't have anything against Him because He hasn't come to you and demanded something you're unwilling to give. But when God comes to you and demands something you're unwilling to give, that's when hostility arises. Whose will is going to win? Yours or His?" That's the struggle every day of the Christian life.

In a previous chapter, I wrote about how to get rid of the nagging the Holy Spirit brings so that we can have peace. And I concluded the only way to do it, is to submit to the prompting of the Holy Spirit. Then, the nagging will go away.

Now, if the Holy Spirit isn't nagging you, you need to quickly make an appointment with your family doctor to see if you're still alive. Surely, the Holy Spirit appeals to everyone. The question is, do you have ears to hear?

Seven times in the book of Revelation, the Bible says, **"Whoever has ears, let them hear what the Spirit says to the churches."** How well do you hear the Spirit? That is the ultimate question.

If you are nagged, if you are uneasy, if you don't have peace, it's because you haven't surrendered your heart to the Spirit. When you surrender, I guarantee that you'll have peace. But it will only come when you submit.

Well, Israel refused to submit; it apostatized over and over again. So, during the week of Christ's death, two wonderful and amazing things happened.

Right before Jesus death, He was riding into Jerusalem on the donkey, and all the children were singing Hosanna to the highest. Jesus gets up to the gates of Jerusalem, stops, tears fill His eyes, and He says, **"If you, even you, had only known on this day what would bring you peace—but now it is hidden from your eyes."**[1]

Shortly before this, speaking to the same Pharisees, He had said, **"Jerusalem, Jerusalem, you who kill the prophets and stone those sent to you, how often I have longed to gather your children together, as a hen gathers her chicks under her wings, and you were not willing. Look, your house is left to you desolate."**[2]

This last verse means that the Spirit of God would never again, corporately, call the house of Israel to repentance. In the verse, Jesus pronounced an irrevocable and eternal sentence upon Israel. Furthermore, because of their obstinacy, destruction would be forthcoming.

A few days later, Jesus was celebrating the Passover with His disciples. He broke the bread and said, **"Take and eat; this is my body."** He then took the wine and puts it into the cup, held it up and said, **"This is my blood of the covenant, which is poured out for many for the forgiveness of sins."**[3]

What Jesus was saying is, "I'm bringing the contract I established with the descendants of Abraham to an end." And on Friday afternoon (when He died), it was consummated. The bilateral contract with the descendants of Abraham was over.

When Jesus died on the cross, He nailed the whole contract to the cross! Now, the unilateral contract God made with Abraham still stands: Abraham will still get the land and be

---

[1] Luke 19:42

[2] Luke 13:34–35

[3] Matthew 26:26–28

the father of many nations; but, Colossians 2 nails the whole bilateral covenant with Abraham's descendants to the cross.

I keep bringing up the question, "Why would any Christian today want to be an heir of Abraham?" Notice what the Bible says, **"If you belong to Christ, then you are Abraham's seed, and heirs according to the promise."**[1] The two things promised to Abraham were just mentioned in the previous paragraph.

Picture in your mind a globe of the world. What God promised Abraham was not a sliver of land in a tiny part of the globe known as the Middle East. That wasn't what God had in mind.

God was not looking to just create one tiny nation, put a few million people in it, and call it "The Land." No, God had a bigger picture in mind. He was going to begin with one man of faith, and this man's family would grow until it, eventually, filled the whole Earth.

What God was offering Abraham was to be the father of MANY nations. And the whole globe is the land to which God is referring; because the day is coming, when, after the land has been purified by fire, it will be given to the heirs of Abraham.

This is why we read in Hebrews 7, there has been a change in the law—meaning the covenant. The Levitical priesthood and the Old Testament laws of Moses were nailed to the cross. Now we have a high priest that comes from the tribe of Judah; and obviously, if your high priest is out of the tribe of JUDAH, you can't be under LEVITICAL law!

It was this understanding, in AD 49, that is recorded in Acts 15, when the new church got together to argue about whether Gentiles should be circumcised or not. And they concluded that the blood covenant had been made void by the death of Christ.

What was the sign of the blood covenant? Circumcision. This meant that circumcision no longer stood for anything. Therefore, it would not be imposed upon the Gentiles.

------

[1] Galatians 3:29

Even though circumcision was declared to be an everlasting sign of the covenant, the fact is, it's only everlasting as long as the blood covenant is in effect. Think of it in terms of the marriage vow. "Till death do us part" is only valid while both parties are alive. When one party dies, the agreement is over.

### Righteousness

I presented earlier that there is a righteousness that comes from God which man has nothing to do with, and this righteousness was created and demonstrated through the life of Christ.

In Drawing 5.2, the record of Jesus' life is illustrated as a book. Jesus lived on Earth 33 years, and the law looks at the life of Christ and declares it to be righteous.

Was there any sin in Jesus? Absolutely not!

So we have, coming from God, a righteousness which you and I cannot produce, cannot emulate, cannot offer. There has never been another person to live on Earth who has done this. No one, other than Jesus, has lived their entire life without sinning.

I am describing a righteousness that comes only from God!

Now, look at the record of my life in Drawing 5.2. My page, in the book of records, looks something like that. The recording angel is documenting my life, and my record has a lot of black lines (which are sins). And so, when God's law looks at my life, it reveals that I'm a sinner.

And what are the wages of sin? Death by execution!

This is why Jesus was executed. This is why the wicked at the end of the one-thousand years will be executed. This is why every lamb which was offered as a sacrifice was executed. No lamb died of old age on the altar. It was killed.

In the Passover, the firstborn lamb was executed because the wages of sin is death by execution. This is what is meant when the Bible says, **"For in the day that thou eatest thereof**

*Drawing 5.2*

**thou shalt surely die.**"[1] This is why Jesus stepped in the way and became man's Intercessor, so that all who would live by faith could be redeemed.

When you are willing to GO wherever God directs, when you are willing to become all that God would have you BE, when you are willing to DO all that God requires—through the Spirit, not the law—you are living by faith.

Living by GO-BE-DO is faith!

Abraham was told to get up and go to a land that he had never seen. "Leave your house, leave your family, gather up your belongings, and go!" Hebrews 11:8 says, he **"obeyed and went, even though he did not know where he was going."**

For all intents and purposes, Abraham could have been wearing a blindfold. It wouldn't have made any difference. But Abraham had ears to hear the Spirit, and when God spoke Abraham responded.

---

[1] Genesis 2:17 KJV

When you live by faith, a wonderful thing happens. When the Father looks at you, He sees in you the righteousness of Christ. He sees you as though you never sinned. And because He sees you in this light, He grants Jesus' righteousness to you.

This is the righteousness we must have in order to be saved, and it only comes through faith. Being a good person won't work. Doing the right things won't get you into heaven.

Previously, I explained the born-again parents who give birth to a carnal baby. The child does all the right things, but conforming to parental expectations doesn't help him one bit.

The born-again experience doesn't happen until the child opens his heart and lets the Spirit in. Being born again is not something we can do by exerting human effort. It doesn't work that way.

Nicodemus said, "Lord, how can a man enter his mother's womb the second time?"[1] Jesus looked at that man and said, "Nicodemus, you, oh great leader of Israel, you don't understand this elementary truth? Whatever is born of Spirit is Spirit. What is born of the flesh is flesh." But, how does one become born again?

### Being Born Again

Read the following sentence carefully because it is perhaps the most important sentence in this book.

*We can only open our heart's door, but God has to perform the miracle!*

What is that miracle? He changes our polarity. Instead of being attracted to evil, He switches the poles so that, like Paul in Romans 7, we begin to love righteousness and hate evil. To be born again is to have our nature transformed so that we can have a taste of oneness with God.

But being born again does not eliminate our carnal nature—it doesn't make us perfect. And it doesn't guarantee that we cannot fall away from God.

---

[1] John 3:4–6

Remember the illustration of the magnet in Drawing 1.1? That switch in polarity is a miracle from God. And it's not a once in a lifetime event. Being born again has to occur every day.

The human heart is like concrete in that it only remains pliable so long. If it hasn't been refreshed with some spiritual indwelling, it will be like concrete by evening, even though it was pure liquid that morning. This is why Paul said, **"I die daily."**[1] He is saying in today's vernacular that, "Living by faith is killing me. Living for Jesus is killing my flesh every day." This is why he declares in Romans 7:15, **"I do not understand what I do. For what I want to do I do not do, but what I hate I do.** [And I don't like it. It's killing me!]**"**

Look at Drawing 5.3.

When a person is born again, he ends up with two natures (carnal and born again) warring against each other. When we're born, the carnal nature comes for free. Everybody reading this understands that.

You can put two little babies in the same room with 50 toys and without exception, in no time at all, they will be fussing over the same toy. This is because the human heart is carnal, selfish, self-centered, and egocentric—everything revolves around us; but, when we're willing to open our hearts to the Holy Spirit, that changes.

Drawing 5.3 reminds me of when, a few years ago during a seminar, I drew an illustration of a man and inadvertently put his heart above his shoulders. Someone told me afterwards that my drawing was anatomically incorrect, that the heart actually goes in the chest! I said, "Let me tell you why I draw it in the throat; because when I'm conducting a seminar, that's where mine is!"

When you open the heart's door and invite the Holy Spirit in, He will come in and change the heart and the affections.

---

[1] 1 Corinthians 15:31 KJV

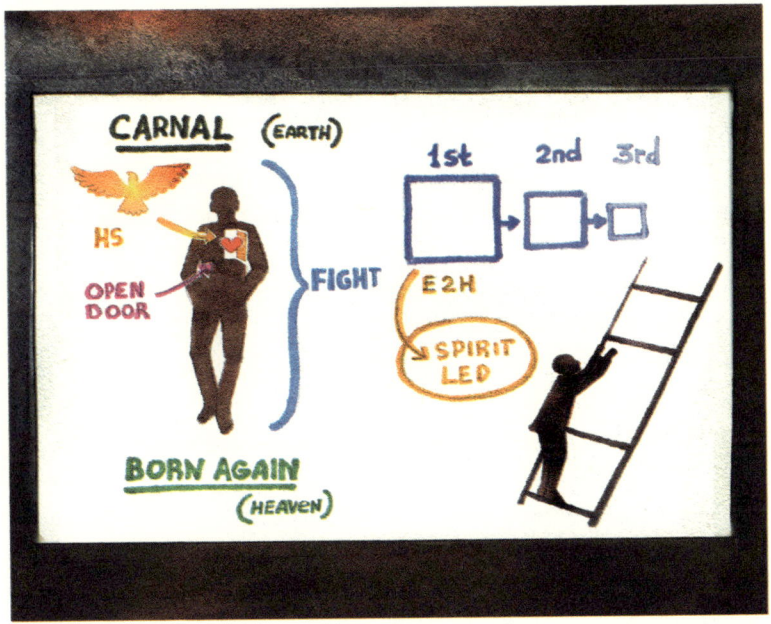

*Drawing 5.3*

The result is that instead of having: your dreams, your goals, your aspirations, your will, your way—you now become interested in knowing what God desires: His will, His dream, His plan, His way.

Afterward, you have what is called the born-again nature. And now, here you are a citizen of both Earth and Heaven having two natures. And these two natures war incessantly. Genesis 3:15 says, **"And I will put enmity between you and the woman, and between your offspring and hers."**

This fight goes on 24–7.

Now, if you don't recognize this fight going on, if you're not experiencing the fight between the two natures, it's because you only have one nature—the carnal nature. And when there's only one nature, self is on the throne, self is in control, self is directing self. But when you're born again, the struggle goes on day after day, and this struggle, Paul says, is to kill the carnal nature.

Most of us are satisfied to acquire a certain level of behavior that is acceptable, and thus, subconsciously, call that our Christian experience. This is where Israel failed time after time.

Read the Old Testament through several times and notice that this is what happens to Israel every time. Israel sets out with good intentions, their hearts born again, their spirits born again, and as long as that generation (1st) is doing whatever they believe to be right, that's enough. But what happens to the second generation (2nd), and the third (3rd)? Well, RIGHT becomes smaller and smaller until somebody in the current generation has ears to hear the Spirit (E2H) and they begin to be Spirit led. Paul makes an interesting point that I didn't understand for many years. In Romans 14:23, he states, **"everything that does not come from faith is sin."** What does this mean?

I believe there is a simple explanation, now that I understand something about *righteousness by faith*. Here's what it means: *If whatever you do is not motivated out of the Spirit-led faith experience—it's of no use. It's worthless. It's garbage.*

Dear friends, the whole heart of the matter is being *born again*. When you become born again, you become born of the Spirit. And if you have ears to hear what the Spirit says, the Spirit will bring you guilt. That's His number one tool. He hits you with guilt; and that nagging—the painful, restless, tormenting remorse—is what motivates you to make wrongs right.

The Spirit is trying to talk to you. The Spirit is trying to say something. He wants you to resolve the nagging. And, to resolve the nagging always has consequences. It always hurts somewhere. But if you will leap out and grab hold of what the Spirit is calling you to do, He will enable you to do the impossible.

This is how we grow in Christ. This is how we are sanctified by faith. It's done by following the Spirit. Like climbing the ladder illustrated in Drawing 5.3, the rung on the ladder to heaven is always an uncomfortable reach.

Imagine you're on the ladder, your arms are extended, and you can't quite reach that next rung. Your reach is one foot short. And in order to get to the next rung, you have to leave the one you're standing on before you can reach the next one.

Living by faith is scary.

Living by faith is a killer.

This is why Israel failed.

It's why most Christians fail. And it's why churches are full of spiritually dead people.

Look at Drawing 5.4.

The Bible predicts a time is coming when the Holy Spirit is going to do a marvelous thing. Until we get to the time when the judgment of the living takes place, the righteousness of Christ has been imputed. Ever since Abel (X) lived and was slain for his fidelity to God, the righteousness of Christ has been imputed.

Imputed is the process where Abel was reckoned as righteous, but in reality, he wasn't. God laid over Abel's life (record) the righteousness of Christ that was to come, and this made Abel righteous.

But a time is coming when the righteousness of Christ is going to be imparted. This means the carnal nature (pink) in all who live by faith is going to be eliminated. The righteousness of Christ will be ours again naturally, just as it was for Adam and Eve in the garden.

The Bible says, **"Then all your people** [children of Abraham] **will be righteous and they will possess the land forever. They are the shoot I have planted, the work of my hands, for the display of my splendor. The least of you will become a thousand, the smallest a mighty nation. I am the Lord; in its time I will do this swiftly."**[1]

---
[1] Isaiah 60:21–22

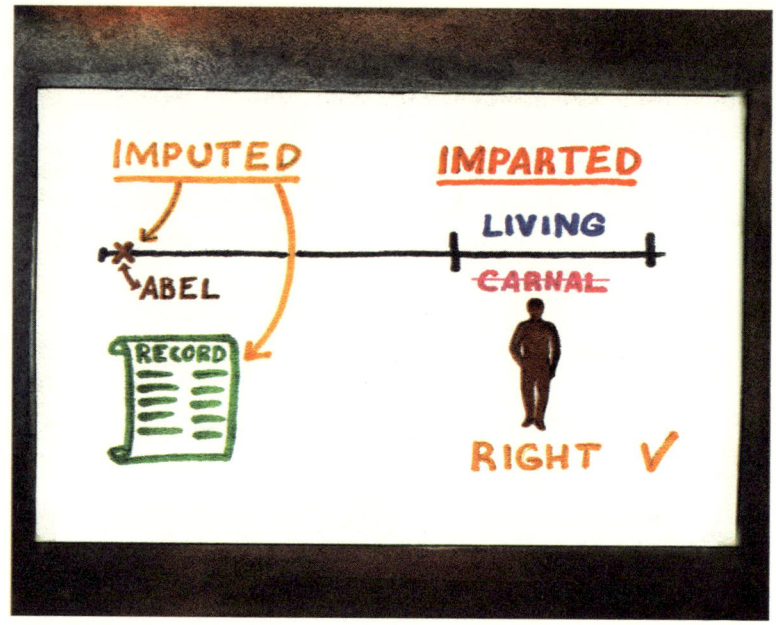

*Drawing 5.4*

Martin Luther, in his search for righteousness by faith, was on the right track. He just didn't follow the track far enough.

Jesus has promised we will be free from the curse of sin at last! Friends, if that doesn't put joy in your soul, you're dead.

As George Younce from the Cathedrals Quartet once said, "If that doesn't light your fire, your wood is wet!"

Pray with me.

Wonderful Father, dear Jesus; eternal God and Savior of man; Lord and Master: thank you for these precious words of encouragement. And as we have this hope in our heart, we want to purify our heart and demonstrate to you that we are willing to follow the Spirit wherever He leads.

We are willing to allow the Spirit to speak. And with the strength and enabling that comes only through you, accomplish all that you want to do through us to your glory and for your honor.

Thank you, dear Lord, for the privilege of knowing your

plans and for the presence of the Holy Spirit. I pray the Spirit will guide and keep us in your presence. In Jesus' name, we pray, amen.

"*When I look at myself, I don't see how I can be saved. But when I look at what Jesus is offering, I don't see how I can be lost.*"

## CHAPTER 6

---

# Truth Will Set You Free

In this chapter, I am going to present something that is quite controversial. Some will like it, and some will hate it. But it doesn't matter. The truth is the truth.

It is imperative we understand truth because the truth sets us free. When Jesus said, "The truth will set you free," He really meant it. It will set you free of your friends, your family, your career, your church membership. Truth is always unfolding, always moving forward, and those who have ears to hear, follow it.

Institutions can neither hear truth nor follow it. One cannot name, historically, a single institution that moved forward with truth. Rather, there are individuals within institutions that step out in faith and truth is confirmed.

Look at what Martin Luther accomplished. I can name a number of reformers: Wycliffe, Hus, Calvin, Knox, Tyndale, the list goes on. Institutions institutionalize. They get boxed in. They can't move forward and this is where they stay.

But people who have ears to hear, always move forward with truth. And I can tell you, moving forward is scary because you never know where you're going. The only thing you know is, you are heaven bound!

In Revelation 7:1, John says, **"After this I saw four angels standing at the four corners of the earth."** Let me explain why he describes his vision this way. Look at Drawing 6.1.

In John's day, Earth was believed to be a flat plate, much like a dinner plate, and there were great fires burning underneath its surface and these were the fires of hell.

It was also understood that a bottomless pit (BP) was a hole that went through Earth's plate; and a volcano was evidence that fires burned and demons lived beneath the earth.

As far as knowledge went in those days, when cartographers drew their maps, they would show oceans as having an edge, believing that if boats sailed out too far they would fall off the edge of the plate into the mouths of ravenous beasts. So when God uses beasts coming up out of the ocean, in John and Daniel's understanding, it is all very much within the body of knowledge they had.

Man did not know that Earth was a sphere until many centuries later. Isaiah spoke about the circle of the Earth, but not of it being a sphere—having volume.

The four corners of Earth are north, south, east, and west. So, God used imagery that John was acquainted with to tell a story. And once you stand in John's sandals to read Revelation, it makes perfect sense just as it reads.

God is not talking to you and me, He was talking to John. God was using imagery John was familiar with so that he could write it down, and then years later, you and I can put on John's sandals and understand the story.

John continues describing what the Lord showed him, **"Holding back the four winds of the earth to prevent any wind from blowing on the land or on the sea or on any tree."**

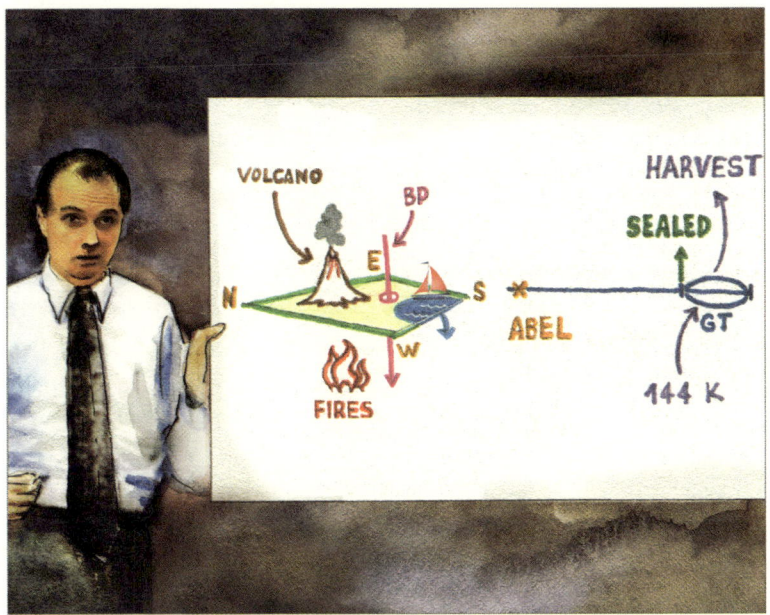

*Drawing 6.1*

The phrase **"any wind"** is important; this means no wind is going to blow until it is time. These four angels are "holding back the four winds of the earth to prevent any wind from blowing on the land, the sea, or any tree."

The Greek word for land is 'ghay', pronounced 'gay.' It is also the word for earth; and the words are used interchangeably. So, whether I'm speaking of the earth or the land, the meaning is the same. The point is that nothing is harmed by these winds until it is time. That's what verse 1 is saying.

Revelation 7:2, **"Then I saw another angel coming up from the east, having the seal of the living God. He called out in a loud voice to the four angels who had been given power to harm the land and the sea:"** So, at this time, these angels had been given power to harm the land, the sea, and the trees.

Revelation 7:3 says, **"Do not harm the land or the sea or the trees until we put a seal on the foreheads of the servants of our God."** This verse tells us two primary things. First, after the servants of God are sealed, harm is coming. Second, the sealing being described is something special that goes on the foreheads of the servants of God. This is not talking about something that has previously happened at any time.

### 144,000

The number of those who are sealed turns out to be 144,000. This is a literal number. There is no such thing in the Bible as a symbolic number. Why would God use one number to represent another number? Besides, if God had declared this to be a symbolic number, the Bible would explain the meaning of the symbol. Otherwise, we would never be able to resolve what the number means.

The fact of the matter is, if you look at Revelation: 5, 6, 7, and 8, you'll find that 12,000 come from the tribe of Judah, 12,000 come from the tribe of Benjamin, etc., and when you add up all the numbers, you actually get the literal number 144,000.

God is going to have 144,000 servants and they are going to be scattered all over the Earth to proclaim the loud cry during the Great Tribulation.

If you divide the population of the world (currently 8 billion) by 144,000, you get a ratio of about 1 servant per 56,000 people.

I believe God loves everybody the same, so He is going to see that everybody gets to hear the gospel. Jesus said in Matthew 24:14, **"And this gospel of the kingdom will be preached in the whole world as a testimony to all nations, and then the end will come."**

Using this 1 to 56,000 ratio, the United States will get about 6,000 of the 144,000 servants. China will get about 26,000 of that group. India, a neighbor to China, will get about 25,000 of the 144,000. I'm just trying to put this in perspective. Revelation's story is not about the United States. It's about this entire world. When Jesus comes, He's not just coming to the United

States. The good news is that Jesus is going to save people all over the world!

In Revelation 7:9, John writes, **"After this I looked, and there before me was a great multitude that no one could count,** [This is a numberless group of people in contrast to the 144,000, which can be counted. And this great multitude comes] **from every nation, tribe, people and language,** [and John sees them] **standing before the throne and before the Lamb. They were wearing white robes and were holding palm branches in their hands."**

This event is obviously after the Second Coming. John is zoomed forward to see a numberless multitude standing before the throne of God, and they are wearing white robes and holding palm branches. Palm branches suggest they have been victorious. White robes indicate righteousness. And, Jesus provided both.

Revelation 7:10, **"And they cried out in a loud voice: 'Salvation belongs to our God, who sits on the throne, and to the Lamb.'"** What they're really saying is, "I didn't work my way to heaven! When Jesus looked at me, He saw me as a sinner. I was found to be unworthy. I do not deserve salvation. Salvation belongs to our God and He has given it to me… undeserving me!" That's what this song is saying.

And the Bible says, **"All the angels were standing around the throne and around the elders and the four living creatures. They fell down on their faces before the throne and worshiped God,"** because of His generosity.[1]

Nothing overwhelms the human heart like a generous gift.

And when the reality of what salvation is worth is seen by this numberless host, they fall on their faces. And they said, **"Amen! Praise and glory and wisdom and thanks and honor and power and strength be to our God for ever and ever. Amen!"**[2] And what this means is that He possesses all of these

---

[1] Revelation 7:11
[2] Revelation 7:12

traits. What else could you attribute to Him that isn't included?

Revelation 7:13–14 says, **"Then one of the** [twenty-four] **elders asked me, 'These in white robes—who are they, and where did they come from?'** I [John, bashfully] **answered, 'Sir, you know.'** [Meaning 'I don't know.'] **And he** [the elder] **said,** [to John] **'These are they who have come out of the great tribulation; they have washed their robes and made them white in the blood of the Lamb.'"**

This is not referring to the redeemed of all the ages. Look at Image 6.1 again.

These people come from a specific point in time. This crowd is not from all those who have lived on Earth since Abel. This is a group gathered out of the Great Tribulation (GT).

The Bible says there is coming a time of trouble, the likes of which has never been since nations were established on Earth.

Daniel 12 talks about this time of trouble. And this is where the great numberless multitude comes from. The Bible says, **"They have washed their robes and made them white in the blood of the Lamb."**[1]

Revelation 7:16–17 expresses something that we need to know about this numberless multitude. **"Never again well they hunger.** [Suggesting they know what hunger is.] **Never again will they thirst.** [Meaning they knew what thirst was.] **The Sun will not beat up on them, nor any scorching heat."** [Suggesting they understood what suffering is.] **For the Lamb at the center of the throne will be their shepherd; 'he will lead them to springs of living water.' 'And God will wipe away every tear from their eyes.'** [Suggesting there were many tears.]"

The 144,000 are in the same chapter as the numberless multitude because they are linked. One group is the mechanism through which God harvests the other group.

You can see on the timeline in Drawing 6.1 when the 144,000 are sealed. The harm to the land and sea and trees

---

[1] Revelation 7:14

commence after they are sealed. And out of the ministry of these 144,000 servants, there will be a harvest so big that it cannot be counted.

The Bible says these servants of God are also prophets.

If you search the phrase "servants the prophets" on one of the web-based Bible platforms (Biblegateway or Biblehub), it will give around 20 verses using that phrase. I'm going to pick several to show you how the phrase is used.

Let's go over to Jeremiah 7:25, where God is speaking through Jeremiah, and He's saying to Israel, **"From the time your ancestors left Egypt until now, day after day, again and again I sent you my servants the prophets."**

Now, go to Jeremiah 25:4. Jeremiah is talking to the people and he says, **"And though the Lord has sent all his servants the prophets to you again and again, you have not listened or paid any attention."**

I'm trying to show you that *Servants the Prophets* is a job title. Sometimes they are called *Servants*, and sometimes they're called *Servants the Prophets*, but it represents those to whom God has commissioned a message to be proclaimed in His name.

Consider who this group is.

In Revelation 7:3, the angel says, **"Do not harm the land or the sea or the trees until we put a seal on the foreheads of the servants of our God."**

These 144,000 are a unique group of people who only exist at one time in Earth's history—at the end. And this group is selected and sealed prior to the harm that is coming.

In Revelation 10:7, the Bible says, **"But in the days when the seventh angel is about to sound his trumpet, the mystery of God will be accomplished, just as he announced to his servants the prophets."**

Let me expound on this.

In Drawing 6.2, the X marks where we are living now. The

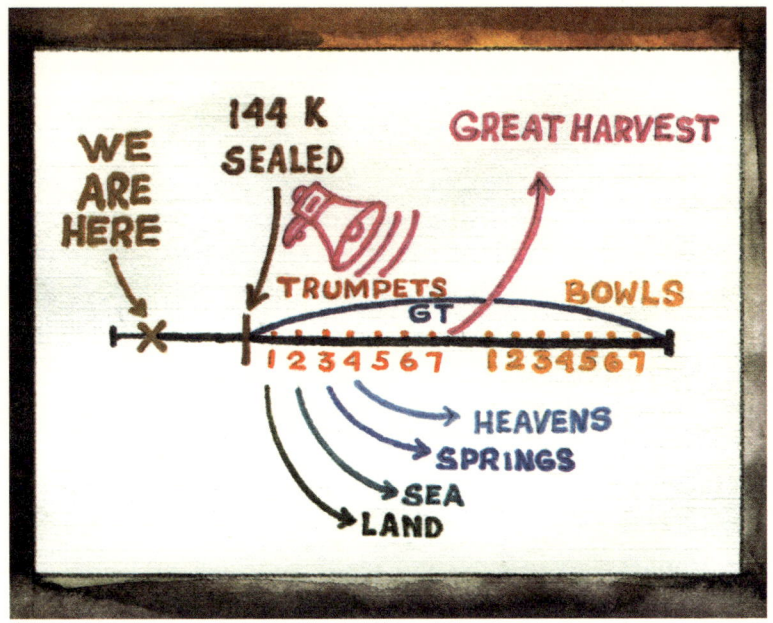

*Drawing 6.2*

vertical line to the right, represents the day when the 144,000
are sealed. After they are sealed, the seven trumpets of Revelation will begin to sound. The first three trumpets harm the
earth, the sea, and the springs through asteroid impacts. The
fourth harms the heavens.

When I first shared the idea that Scripture teaches God
is going to impact Earth with great manifestations from the
heavens, people questioned my sanity. Today, the threat of an
asteroid impact is serious business. Hollywood has released
movies about asteroids impacting Earth and the devastation
they will cause. But God's Word has contained this informa-
tion for two-thousand years; and I am by no means the first to
reach this conclusion.

God is going to devastate this Earth to get everyone's undivided attention. He is going to distress it with a time of trouble
called the Great Tribulation (GT). During this time period, the
144,000 are going to proclaim the gospel of Jesus with great

power and authority, and a great multitude that no one can count will be the harvest.

What this means is each one of us has a chance! Think about it. If the harvest was only thirteen people, what would our hope be? We would have a problem. The good news is, the redeemed are going to be a numberless multitude!

A billion is one-thousand-million. Currently on Earth, there are eight-thousand-million people! The mystery of God is, anybody can be saved! The good news is, He can and will save a wretch like me; all I have to do is live by faith. Consider what all this means.

God is going to save people of every nation, kindred, tongue, and people. He is going to save Muslims, Jews, Catholics, Protestants, Hindus, and even heathen. And the way He accomplishes this is, He's going to select and send 144,000 servants throughout the Earth.

The first message that the 144,000 will proclaim (with a bullhorn) is found in Revelation 14:6. It's represented to John as an angel flying in midair, indicating the angel is flying above the earth. The verse says, **"Then I saw another angel flying in midair, and he had the eternal gospel to proclaim to those who live on the earth—to every nation, tribe, language and people."**

The word angel comes from the Greek word 'aggelos' which really means 'messenger.' It is transliterated 'angel' because it is flying in midair. But the verse really means, "I saw another messenger flying in midair, and he had the eternal gospel."

What is the eternal gospel? It is, *the just shall live by faith.* You can read that in Habakkuk 2, Romans 1, Galatians 3, and Hebrews 10.

Revelation 14:7 says, **"He** [the angel] **said in a loud voice, 'Fear God and give him glory, because the hour of his judgment has come. Worship him who made the heavens, the earth, the sea and the springs of water.'"**

I need to explain this.

The first trumpet harms *the land*. This trumpet is a great meteoric shower of burning hail that sets the whole world on fire. Look on YouTube at some of the great fires that have burned through California. It will give you a visual of the ferocity of the fires caused by the first trumpet. Tens of thousands of people are trying to get out of these California cities and the freeways are paralyzed.

The second trumpet harms *the sea*. An asteroid hits an ocean and a third of the sea creatures die; a third the ships are sunk; a third of the sea turns to blood.

The third trumpet harms *the springs of water*. Another asteroid impact, which strikes a landmass, sends shockwaves throughout the earth. The shockwaves sever aquifers, water systems, sewer systems, and septic leaching fields. Then, people unknowingly drink the contaminated water and die.

The fourth trumpet harms *the sun, moon, and stars*.

Every year, our world passes through nine different meteor showers. And there is great concern that projectiles from the cosmic debris will render some of our multi-million dollar satellites totally inoperable and useless.

Today, we have about 6,000 satellites in orbit around the Earth, and this cosmic debris is moving toward Earth at about 80,000 miles per hour. As our globe spins and rotates, we're moving toward the debris at about 72,000 miles per hour. This represents a 152,000 mile per hour collision!

And these tiny specs of meteoroids, acting like thimble sized missiles, traveling at warp speed, will go through a satellite and never even notice it. Then, as these little projectiles enter the atmosphere, they turn into white-hot falling rocks and pepper the Earth with fire.

The first four trumpets bring about incredible devastation all over the world. This is how God will get the undivided attention of 8 billion people, or what remains of them.

Notice the first angel's message (and command) in Revelation 14:7. **"Worship him who made the heavens, the earth, the sea and the springs of water."** (Refer to Drawing 6.2)

The sun, moon, and stars (heavens) are the items affected in the fourth trumpet; the earth (land) is affected in the first trumpet; the sea in the second trumpet; and springs of water in the third trumpet.

The verse is saying, "Worship God, the creator, who has just devastated these things." That's really what this is all about.

"For the hour of the judgment of the living has come." The judgment of the living happens during the trumpet period being described.

In Old Testament times, beginning on the first day of the seventh month, trumpets began blowing to celebrate the Feast of Trumpets. And the whole point of this sounding of the trumpets for nine days was to remind Israel that the Day of Atonement was coming, so get ready to be right with God.

This sounding of the trumpets was to awaken God's people (Israel) to the fact that mercy was coming to a close. Sacrifices for sin were no longer possible after the ninth day of the seventh month. It was over. It was finished.

The close of probation never caught Israel by surprise. The Day of Atonement always began on the tenth day of the seventh month each year.[1] God generously had the trumpets sound so that if anyone had unconfessed sins, they could take care of them before mercy ended.

In the same way, God is going to sound the trumpets of Revelation. The purpose of the seven trumpets is to awaken a world to the reality that God's mercy is coming to a close.

We just read in Revelation 10:7, **"But in the days when the seventh angel is about to sound his trumpet, the mystery of God will be accomplished, just as he announced to his servants the prophets."**

---

[1] Leviticus 23:27

The plan is very simple. You may not believe it, but that doesn't matter. In Noah's day, all but eight people voted for no flood. It happened anyway.

What God has declared, He will do. We cannot stop it. We cannot prohibit it. We cannot prevent it. The clock is ticking. It is coming. All we can do is be ready. This is why we have His Word, so we can study it and understand His plans. We need to be ready.

Look at Drawing 6.3. The 7 trumpets are a time period of mercy. The 7 bowls are a time period of no mercy. So, we have 7 first plagues and 7 last plagues—14 events in all. The Second Coming of Jesus (cloud) is during the seventh bowl.

During the time period of the 7 trumpets, the Holy Spirit is going to be poured out on all mankind to redeem a numberless multitude. Joel 2:28 says, **"And afterward, I will pour out my Spirit on all people."** The first people to receive the empowerment and all that the Holy Spirit has to offer will be the firstfruits—the 144,000. They're first to be sealed.

Now, if I grow watermelons, what will my firstfruits be? Watermelons. If I grow and harvest apples, what will my firstfruits be? Apples. If the harvest consists of people from every nation, kindred, tongue, and people, from where will the firstfruits come? From every nation, kindred, tongue, and people. If the harvest comes from China, Russia, and Africa, will there be firstfruits from these places? Yes!

What I'm trying to get you to see is that God will have spokespersons on every continent, in every nation, who will speak for Him. The 144,000 will come from every tribe, language, and nation because the harvest comes from every tribe, language, and nation.

Here's the bottom line. Every person is going to take the test of faith.

First, everyone is going to hear the gospel.

Second, everyone is going to make a decision about whether

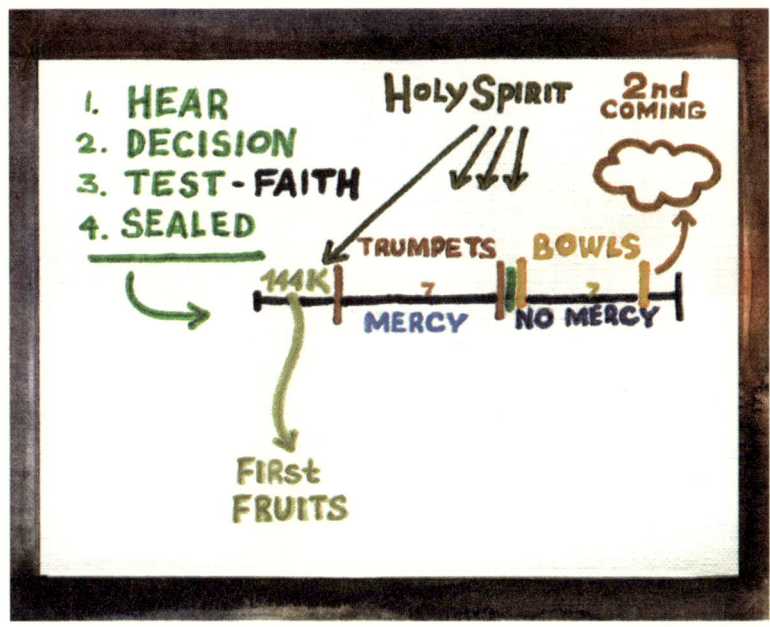

*Drawing 6.3*

or not they will receive the gospel and obey the command to worship God on His holy Sabbath day. The first angel's message is, **"Worship him who made the heavens, the earth, the sea and the springs of water."**

Third, everyone on Earth is going to be tested to see what their faith is.

And last, everyone will be sealed in his decision.

*Righteousness of Christ*

Now, here's the good news! The sealing is when God removes the carnal nature from all who live by faith and gives them a new nature. This will happen before the close of mercy and the seven last plagues commence.

When God does this, His people will no longer need an intercessor because they'll have no attraction for sin. No longer will the fight and the struggle with sin go on. It will be over. Jesus said, **"Let the one who does wrong continue to do wrong; let the vile person continue to be vile; let the one** who does right continue to do right; and let the holy person continue to be holy."

Now look at 1 John 3:2. I love this text. **"Dear friends, now we are children of God, and what we will be has not yet been made known. But we know that when Christ appears, we shall be like him, for we shall see him as he is."**

In other words, we haven't seen Him as He is yet; but we know that when He appears, we shall be just like Him. Moses wanted to see the face of God; and God said, "No Moses, you can't see me or you will die. No one can see me. No sinner can see my face and live. But, I will do this for you. I'll hide you in the cleft of the rock and let my goodness pass in front of you."[1]

The Bible says, this was such a glorious experience for Moses, that when he came down from the mountain, he had to put a veil over his glowing face so as not to frighten the people.[2]

But John is saying, **"We shall be like him."** We shall see Jesus face to face. This means the carnal nature is gone. We'll be free! God is going to remove the carnal nature from those who pass the test of faith. What a wonderful thought.

Now, let's delve into what 'walking by faith' looks like experientially. Walking by faith usually ends up placing one's whole life experience in a tiny closet. The lights are out. It's dark. We don't know which way to go. We can't go forward or backward. We can't turn left or right. We're frustrated. We're frozen like the children of Israel just after they left Egypt, and Pharaoh's army is coming. The sea is ahead, scorching desert to the west, impassable mountains to the east, an angry pharaoh is coming from the south. Where can we turn? Where can we go?

James 1:2–3 says, "When we find ourselves in this predicament, count it all joy." He says this because, it's only when we are in a desperate situation that we really appreciate God's deliverance.

When we live by faith, we're always putting ourselves

---

[1] Exodus 33:18–23
[2] Exodus 35:29–35

at God's mercy as He leads us by the Spirit, as He speaks to our hearts, as He compels us. And, as we go forward, there is always trouble—always consequences. But this is how God reveals Himself.

We marvel at Bible stories such as *Daniel in the Lion's Den* and *Shadrach, Meshach, and Abednego*. But after reading these stories, we soon realize that the only way God's marvelous works can be revealed is through those who live by faith. That's the way it has to be. And so, God likes to lead us out on a limb and cut the limb off, then, take hold of our hand and lift us up.

*Why 1844 is Important*

I would like to explain something that hasn't been addressed yet, so that we're on the same page. It is my understanding that, in 1844, God commenced a special process in heaven. Speaking of this time period, Daniel 7:10 says that, **"The court was seated, and the books were opened."** Let me explain what is going on in this court room setting.

I understand from Scripture and from prophecy that there is a pre-advent judgment which comes in two flavors: one for the dead, and one for the living. You can see the two time periods in Drawing 6.4.

In the judgment of the dead, God has some books of record in heaven. The Bible says, we shall all stand before the judgment seat of Christ that we might receive what we have done while in the body, whether it is good or bad.

Notice in Drawing 6.4, a book of record. I use this to illustrate how our lives are being recorded by angels. Very specific angels have been commissioned by God to record our entire life's story. And these angels will not only record our actions, but our thoughts and motives as well. This is being done, and has been done, for all who have ever lived.

Solomon says in Ecclesiastes 12:14, **"For God will bring every deed into judgment, including every hidden thing, whether it is good or evil."** This means, there is a judgment

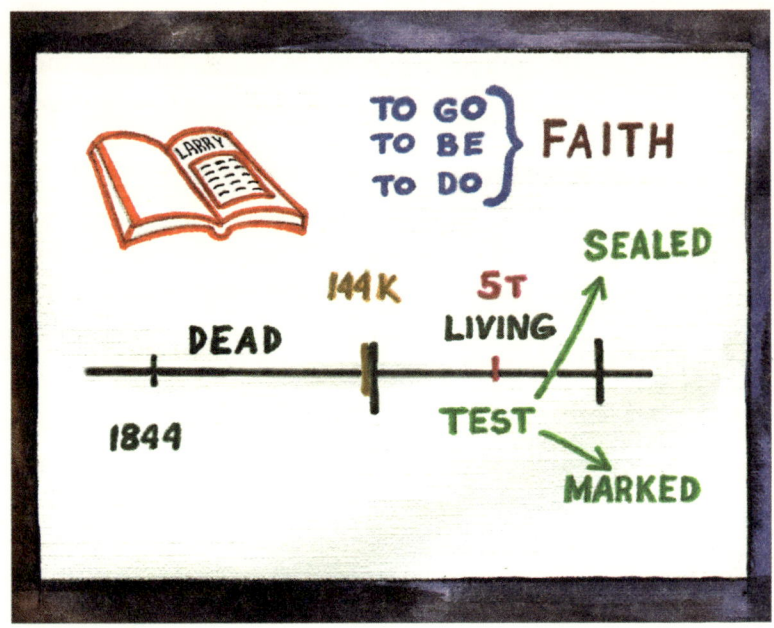

*Drawing 6.4*

day coming.

In the English language, we have the word *infinity* which means something that is ever ongoing or without end. That is my understanding of how living by faith works, and why I say that living by faith is to go, to be, and to do. It's ever ongoing. When you live by faith, it never stops. And, it will NEVER stop throughout eternity.

When we give our lives to the Lord, we surrender all. Wouldn't it be awful to be given an assignment that takes 33,000 years, and we don't want to do it because our heart isn't in it? Can you imagine God having you repaint the Grand Canyon with a toothbrush, and you don't like to paint?

Heaven is not a democracy. People don't vote there. God is a dictator: the most benevolent and loving dictator, you will ever know. When God asks you to do something, He will prepare and equip you to do it; and it will be your greatest joy, because it will fit you for how you really are.

God understands our unique DNA. No two of us see things the same way, nor do we value the same things. We are all different. God knows it. The Bible says, He even knows the number of hairs on our heads, and for me, that's a changing number every day!

I never considered that preaching the gospel would make me happy until I gave my life to the Lord and He called me. He knew what would make me happy and what it would take. I had my own ideas, my own agenda, my own plans.

### Judgment of the Dead

In the judgment of the dead, for the person who lives by faith, the righteousness of Christ is laid over their life. This is called imputed righteousness.

I believe the first person Jesus judged was Abel, because he was the first person to become un-able. And as we go down through history, during this judgment process, Jesus is simply going through the books of record, and as He comes to each page, there is only one question is asked: Does this person have the covering of Christ's righteousness?

If he has, then it doesn't matter if he's the thief on the cross. It doesn't matter how many evil things he has done. It doesn't matter what a wretch he's been. It doesn't matter! What matters is, does he have the righteousness of Christ?

This is not all that takes place in the judgment, but it is all that has to do with whether we have salvation or not. Now, let me explain the rest of the story.

### Jesus Explains Why

After everyone's righteousness has been determined, Jesus then addresses the angels who are standing around the throne. After having observed the judgment process, Jesus is going to explain to them what He has done and why.

I'll use my life to illustrate what takes place.

First, Jesus removes the covering of His righteousness from

my record and holds up what the angels actually recorded so all can see my shame. Jesus then points out why—and defends why—as man's Judge, He gave me His righteousness. He does this because, as my Advocate, He wants them to understand why He redeemed me. Salvation is not a whitewash, it never has been.

You must understand the position Christ is in. He wears two hats. On one side, He is the Defender of God's law; on the other, He's the Advocate of man. He must uphold and demonstrate the integrity of God's law, AND show that giving Larry His righteousness is appropriate because Larry lived by faith.

Remember, the stipulation is, all who live by faith will receive Christ's righteousness. So Christ is going to defend before the presence of the angels and twenty-four elders how He knew it would be appropriate.

This is why God convened the hosts of heaven. He wants them to understand the integrity of the process and see that Jesus is not saving friends, He's complying with law.

The law and the plan of salvation stipulate that a man can be saved, will be saved, by faith. And after Jesus' explanation, the Bible says, the angels and the twenty-four elders say, amen.

What this means is that when you and I walk the golden streets, the angels, who will know all that they want to know about us and more, will never have any question about our being there, because they have seen our life, they have seen our faith, and they have seen the generosity of God.

This is important because God's children, when they're in the Earth made new, are going to be on a level above the angels. We will be a kingdom of priests and a holy nation—a holy race dedicated to serving our God—and we will be higher in our service then that of the angels.

I know this because Jesus came down to Earth and took on our humanity; and in stooping down to identify with us, He has lifted us above all others for eternity. For none of the other created beings, throughout God's universe, will share in the same identity we will share with Christ. This is why the 144,000 are firstfruits.

In the Old Testament, every time firstfruits were presented, they belonged to the high priest; they were his special property—exclusively! The other priests did not get firstfruits.

The 144,000 will be a special entourage who follow Christ wherever He goes throughout the universe because they are His personal property. They are HIS firstfruits.

God has lifted us up and exalted the worst of His creation. We're the only race that has fallen. We're the only world that has sinned. God has lifted us up through Christ to the highest place in heaven.

And the wisdom of God in doing this is wonderful because He is going to have, throughout billions of light years, a race of people who understand the knowledge of good and evil; who understand what sin is all about because they've *been there and done that*. God will have a people throughout the universe who can explain His love, His patience, His forbearance, and defend His wisdom.

Here's the problem. When you live with a being who is infinite, you can never fully understand Him. He may do something today that takes ten-thousand years to understand. So how are we supposed to live in harmony with Him? The only way is through faith.

When Adam and Eve sinned and Jesus interceded, the angels were scratching their heads wondering what was going on because the pair weren't killed as had been promised. It's taken six-thousand years for this to play out. This is why He calls them all together in the judgment—to explain what He's doing and why so they can understand.

The only way we can live with God and be happy, is to accept that: A) God does no wrong; B) God is perfect and righteous in all that He is doing; and C) His wisdom will be proven to be best in the end. We have no option but to hang on by faith and go forward, trusting it'll all work out in the end. That's why salvation comes by faith. We have already seen what happens when we don't trust God. Lucifer didn't trust God and we know how that turned out.

In John 5:22, the Bible says, "**The Father judges no one, but has entrusted all judgment to the Son.**" Hebrews 4:14–15 says, "**We have a great high priest who has ascended into heaven… one who has been tempted in every way, just as we are.**" Jesus knows what it's like. We have an Advocate, and He's a wonderful Friend and Savior.

I have just described what takes place in the judgment of the dead. The judgment of the living, however, is handled differently. Let me explain how the living are judged. Their process doesn't include books of record. Although angels are recording each life, the records aren't used to judge the living.

In the judgment of the living process, the living judge themselves. Here's why. It would be unfair of God to judge us while we are living, if judgment were based on written records, because we're not finished yet. We're still living. Our records aren't complete. God would be predetermining our destiny for us, if we haven't finished living our lives to indicate our choice.

If God just steps in and declares this or that, but we still have more life to live, well, who knows, we may change our mind a month from now. You see the problem?

Revelation 3:10 says, "**Since you have kept my command to endure patiently, I will also keep you from the hour of trial that is going to come on the whole world to test the inhabitants of the earth.**"

Notice on the timeline in Drawing 6.4 that God is going to test the living; and this test has two options: either you receive the mark of the beast or you receive the seal of God. Everyone ends up with one or the other.

The process of judging the living begins in the house of God.

The first to be judged will be the 144,000. This happens before the devastations commence. As we go through the judgment of the living, we reach a plateau at the fifth trumpet (5T) where most of the world will have made their decision for or against the gospel.

The devil will be released during the fifth trumpet and physically appear on Earth claiming to be God. The Bible says, in Revelation 9:4–6, that he will torture those not having the seal of God, and the torture is so bad that people long to die but can't. God releases the devil and allows him to physically appear because: 1) people have refused to believe the truth; and 2) so that some, even in their suffering, will listen and be saved.

The story in Numbers 21—when Israel apostatized and God sent millions of snakes into the camp—snakes were in their tents, their bedding, everywhere, and the people were dying. The Bible says, **"The Lord said to Moses, 'Make a snake and put it up on a pole; anyone who is bitten can look at it and live.' So Moses made a bronze snake and put it up on a pole. Then when anyone was bitten by a snake and looked at the bronze snake, they lived."**[1]

It took faith to go and look at the snake on the pole, because once you've been bitten by a poisonous snake, you want to be as still as possible. You don't want to accelerate the heart; you want to shut down the circulation so that the venom is kept as local as possible.

Well, it was about one mile from the sanctuary in the middle of the camp out to where the tents were, and getting over there to see that snake on the bronze pole was truly an act of faith. If you were bitten, you had quite a hike to get to the bronze serpent.

God used this object lesson to show Israel that we have all been bitten by the serpent of sin. And if we will, in faith, look up to the One who would be made sin for us, we can be saved.

---

[1] Numbers 21:8–9

Jesus is symbolized as a serpent to represent what He would bear and become for us. Paul says in 2 Corinthians 5:21, **"God made him who had no sin to be sin for us."**

God will allow the devil to inflict torment during the fifth trumpet so that, if possible, those who are suffering might find a Savior. The purpose of the trumpets is to notify the world: "Get ready to meet your Maker. Salvation is coming to a close. Prepare to meet God." I think it is so neat how God even uses this vile situation to save to the utmost.

In Galatians 5, Paul knew the day was coming when the carnal nature would be removed. But remember, Paul died about 30 years before the book of Revelation was given. God wasn't through talking. Paul didn't hear the whole story. No one prophet knew the whole story. The book of Daniel was locked until the time of the end, so there are things in Daniel that Peter, James, and John could not know.

Notice what Galatians 5:5 says, **"For through the Spirit we eagerly await by faith the righteousness for which we hope."** Paul knew that God had promised—on covenant—that He would change our nature.

The author of Hebrews writes, **"This is the covenant I will establish with the people of Israel after that time, declares the Lord. I will put my laws in their minds and write them on their hearts. I will be their God, and they will be my people."**[1] This means that rebellion will no longer be in us. The righteousness of Christ will be imparted. No more rebellion.

Currently, there's rebellion within us—we all have it. But the day is coming when God is going to change that. And the good news is, it happens before the close of mercy. When Jesus finishes His mediatorial work, it's over. And it will never resume—EVER. Sin will never rise again. It will be finished.

This is when Jesus declares: **"Let the one who does wrong continue to do wrong; let the vile person continue to be vile;**

---

[1] Hebrews 8:10

let the one who does right continue to do right; and let the holy person continue to be holy."[1]

What He's saying is found in Hebrews 8:10–11, "**I will be their God, and they will be my people.** [because they will be like I am] **No longer will they teach their neighbor, or say to one another, 'Know the Lord,' because…**" it's over. There is no more need for evangelism; there is no more need for preachers; there is no more need for proclaiming, "Know the Lord." It's over!

And this is confirmed in Revelation 10:7, "**But in the days when the seventh angel is about to sound his trumpet, the mystery of God will be accomplished.**" Paul says about the mystery of God, "**My goal is that they may be encouraged in heart and united in love, so that they may have the full riches of complete understanding, in order that they may know the mystery of God, namely, Christ.**"[2]

In Colossians 1:27, he is writing to the saints and says, "**To them God has chosen to make known among the Gentiles the glorious riches of this mystery, which is Christ in you, the hope of glory.**" Did you notice what the mystery is? "**Christ in you.**"

The more we understand about righteousness by faith, the more we can understand what Paul is saying. *The mystery of God is Christ's righteousness imparted to us.*

John says in 1 John 3:2, "**Dear friends, now we are children of God, and what we will be has not yet been made known. But we know that when Christ appears, we shall be like him, for we shall see him as he is.**" Did you notice that when He appears, "We shall be like him?"

Just before Christ's righteousness is imparted, everyone is going to hear the gospel, make a decision for or against the gospel, be tested in that decision, and then, as a result of the test, sealed or marked according to their decision.

---

[1] Revelation 22:11

[2] Colossians 2:2

Revelation 10:7 says, **"But in the days when the seventh angle is about to sound his trumpet, the mystery of God will be accomplished, just as he announced to his servants the prophets."** And the mystery of God is this... **"Christ in you."** His laws and ways will be written in our hearts and sealed forever.

God is going to preserve His Spirit within us. He's going to seal us. This is how the Saints will go through the seven last plagues without any fear of sinning. This is how the saints go through that time period waiting for the Lord without worrying about offending their Lord. At this point in the process, we've been changed—we've been sealed!

When Jesus Christ appears in the clouds of glory, we shall see Him as He is. We shall look upon His face! We shall jump for joy! And our bodies shall be changed. The mortal will put on immortality and the corruption will be gone—forever more. I can hardly wait! But, until the Lord comes, I continue to press on... and so must you.

# CHAPTER 7

# Going Home

It was my prayer, when I began putting this manuscript together, that all who read this would be blessed with knowing the Lord better. I hope you do.

Up to this point, while looking and examining and studying God's Word, we've covered: justification and sanctification, how to overcome sin, how to listen to the Spirit, how to follow the Spirit, and how to claim the power of God. I have tried to explain the blood covenant, how we're under a new covenant whose Mediator is Christ, and how the covenant we're most concerned with is the unilateral covenant given to Abraham.

The reason God's promise to Abraham is so important is that the land and life eternal promised will go to all of Abraham's spiritual offspring.

We understand from Romans 9, Ephesians 2, and Galatians 3, that those who live by faith are the offspring of Abraham; that in Christ, there is neither Jew nor Gentile, slave nor free, male nor female. And we know this male and female business is important because, under the Levitical system, females could not enter into the temple—they had to stay outside.

God did this to show that He held the male responsible for the spiritual well-being of his family. Unfortunately, today, many men do not understand or take this responsibility seriously. But it is a responsibility that the Spirit will lay on the heart of a husband who loves his wife as Christ loves His church.

### End-Times

The following conclusions may be different from what you presently understand, but at least consider them. If we are accustomed to hearing the Spirit's voice, He will tell us what truth is and is not.

If we have ears to hear, the Spirit bears witness from within and we know it is correct. Even if we initially misunderstand the leading of the Spirit, He will come back and make sure we get it right. That's the way He works.

I haven't always understood things the way I do currently. And in my search for truth, I'm sure I will change my mind on certain things. As students of God's Word, we should be open to change. It's the only way to grow.

I am a pupil, not an authority. It isn't my place to tell you what to believe, only to share what God has impressed upon my heart. In John 16:13, Jesus said, **"But when he, the Spirit of truth, comes, he will guide you into all the truth."** This is a never-ending journey.

In Joel 2:28–31, God gave a prophecy where He promised, in the last days, to pour out His Spirit on everybody, everywhere. That means ALL people. **"And afterward, I will pour out my Spirit on all people. Your sons and daughters will prophesy, your old men will dream dreams, your young men will see visions."**

If there are 8 billion people on the planet, God is going to pour His Spirit out on all of them. We are about to enter a time period of the *Dispensation of the Holy Spirit.*

According to Scripture, this outpouring lasts only 1,260 days and will accommodate the work of God's *servants the prophets.* **"I will pour out my Spirit on all people...Even on my servants, both men and women** [because in Christ, there is no difference. The 144,000 will be made up of men and women, and on both of them], **I will pour out my Spirit in those days. I will show wonders in the heavens and on the earth, blood and fire and billows of smoke. The sun will be turned to darkness and the moon to blood before the coming of the great and dreadful day of the Lord."**

Look at Drawing 7.1. I can't discuss much without a timeline to give perspective of where I am going. Previously, I presented the sealing of the 144,000. Their sealing occurs before the harm begins (arrow). God is going to pour out His Spirit on His servants.

And we know the 144,000 will be sealed FIRST because they're firstfruits.[1] Then, God is going to pour out the Holy Spirit on everybody everywhere, so that, as His servants go forward proclaiming the three angels' messages, everyone will hear what He has to say. And after the three angel's proclaim their messages, a fourth angel amplifies all that has been said by the previous three.

Notice what Jesus said to His disciples in John 16:13. **"But when he, the Spirit of truth, comes, he will guide you into all the truth."** Now carefully notice the next phrase, **"He will not speak on his own; he will speak only what he hears, and he will tell you what is yet to come."**

If the Spirit wanted to, He could speak on His own—because the Spirit is God. He's one of the Godhead. He has all the authority, all the prerogatives, all the power the Father and Son have. Yet the verse says, **"He will not speak on his own; he will speak only what he hears, and he will tell you what is yet to come."**

---

[1] Revelation 14

In Drawing 7.1, Jesus is sitting on His throne with a crown on His head. When Jesus speaks to the Holy Spirit, the Holy Spirit hears and then delivers the message to the servants. You can see the servants, both men and women, receiving the message. This will be a special phenomenon.

God is going to have servants all over the world, and most of these people will not know each other or have anything in common—no language, no culture, no religion. These people will have only one thing in common, and that is God has chosen them to serve Him because they live by faith.

God has people who love Him supremely in every culture, and I anticipate the 144,000 will come out of every religious body. I believe God is going to choose some Muslims, Jews, Hindus, Protestants, Catholics, even some heathen (as Christians call non-Christians). God is going to choose people from every religious group on the planet, and these people will be His servants.

Every church I know of (that has a prophetic position) believes the 144,000 will spring from itself. I run into this everywhere I go, no matter the denomination. If a church has a position on prophecy, it always appropriates itself as being central to God's closing events.

I confess, I used to be that way. I saw my church and myself center-stage of finishing God's great work, sort of like Abraham and Sarah contriving a plan to help God deliver the child of promise. But that all melted away for me when I finally realized that only God can do the impossible. Let me explain.

What would be the likelihood of a Jew going to a Muslim and saying, "Know the Lord"?

What would be the possibility of a Muslim leading a Jew into truth?

What would be the possibility of a Jew convincing you that his religious views were correct?

What would be the possibility of a Muslim convincing you

*Drawing 7.1*

of his view of God?

It isn't possible. There are 8 billion people on this planet and about 1.9 billion are Muslim; it's the largest religious organization on the planet. There are about 1.2 billion Hindu, about 1.3 billion Catholics, and about 800 million Protestants.

We live in a divided world. God Himself made it divided at the Tower of Babel. He split the languages, sent people off into groups, then pulled the Earth apart, and there they were stuck. God has a world full of people, and there are devout children in every religious system.

Let me use a Muslim country to illustrate what the Lord is going to do according to Scripture. Now, understand, because the people in my illustration are pure in heart, because of their faith and living up to all they know to be right and true, God considers them His children.

Paul says in Romans 2:14, **"When Gentiles, who do not have the law, do by nature things required by the law."** And

John says, "**For God so loved the WORLD that he gave his only begotten Son.**"[1] God loves the WHOLE world, not just the United States of America.

So, for my illustration, suppose God chooses 30,000 Muslims and gives them the first angel's message. Well, because they're already led by the Spirit, they will love it. Then when the harm begins, they will be prepositioned and ready to speak to their Muslim brothers.

Who better to do this than brothers? They already understand the culture, the religion, the way of life. What God is doing is showing that His salvation is extended to anyone who will live by faith.

The FIRST ANGEL'S MESSAGE is a call to worship God; and the command to worship God includes worshiping God on His Sabbath day. There is no other way to worship God. He has given us, in His commandments, instructions on how to worship Him; and the amazing thing is, there are going to be Muslim brothers telling Muslim brothers, 'keep the Sabbath.'

In Revelation 7:9, John says that a numberless multitude "**from every nation, tribe, people and language**" comes out of the Great Tribulation. No church can do the work that has to be done. None. Only God can do what has to be done. There will be Muslims talking to Muslims, Jews talking to Jews, Catholics talking to Catholics, Protestants talking to Protestants.

During the Great Tribulation, when the religious leaders of the world see the enormous devastation, they will conclude God is angry—that He has reached His limit of patience. And because God is angry and expressing His wrath, what do you think the religions of the world will do to make it stop?

It depends on where you live. Muslims observe Friday as a holy day. Jews observe Saturday. Christians predominately observe Sunday. There are some Christians who observe Saturday but, as a percentage, not very many.

---

1 John 3:16

When God's wrath is unleashed and these worldwide judgments occur, the religions of the world that have a holy day will immediately set up laws regarding the worship of God. Think about it. The destruction is worldwide.

The first trumpet burns up one-third of the trees and all of the green grass on the planet. The first asteroid impact hits one of the oceans and wipes out all of the coastal cities surrounding that ocean.

When you take something one mile in diameter, sailing through space at 40,000 miles per hour, and drop it into an ocean, you're going to create a big splash!

The Bible says, when this happens, one-third of the ships will be sunk! Notice what Luke 21:25 says about this time period: **"There will be signs in the sun, moon and stars. On the earth, nations will be in anguish and perplexity at the roaring and tossing of the sea."**

What will have the sea in dire commotion? A big impact.

There is abundant evidence of asteroid impacts over the face of the Earth. In fact, you can go out tonight and look up at the moon and clearly see what impacts look like.

When the Shoemaker-Levy 9 comet impacted Jupiter during July of '94, one of the twenty-one pieces that plowed into Jupiter left a hole 7,500 miles wide! That hole was as big as the Pacific Ocean. That's a big hole! And it was just one of the twenty-one pieces that hit Jupiter.

My point is that when these judgments come, the religions of the world having a holy day will immediately set up laws governing worship. There will be Friday laws, Saturday laws, and Sunday laws depending on what part of the world one lives in.

These *sin-less* laws will be designed to appease God. The idea is to do less sinning in an effort to make God stop His wrath. The religious leaders will insist their governments coerce people to comply. Martial law will be implemented. When this happens, wherever you are, you will be stuck.

During martial law, you can't go wherever you want. You can't go to your home; you are forbidden on the order of law. Those who have experienced martial law, and lived to tell about it, know what I am saying is true.

When the religious leaders tell the political authorities, "This is the wrath of God, and the only way to stop this is to make laws reverencing God." It is in this context laws on each of the respective days of worship will be made.

The neat thing is, God will have His servants telling people, "No, this isn't what God wants. God wants to be worshiped. Worship the Creator on His holy day, which is Saturday."

This will put those who follow the Spirit in direct opposition to the laws of the land. Those who follow the Holy Spirit will be persecuted. Penalties will be swift and severe. In Israel, where the Sabbath is already regarded as God's holy day, there will be an interesting twist because God will have His Jewish servants telling other Jews to worship Christ—the Creator. This will be a very different but severe problem as well.

The Bible says in Revelation 12:17, **"Then the dragon was enraged at the woman and went off to wage war against the rest** [or the last, or the remnant] **of her offspring."** And the offspring are identified as having two properties: **"Those who keep God's commands and hold fast their testimony about Jesus."**

The two things that will identify God's people are: 1) those who obey God's commands, and 2) hold fast to His testimony. What is the testimony of Jesus?

In Revelation 19:10, we find that the testimony of Jesus is the Spirit of prophecy. There are at least ten church denominations I know of that claim to have the Spirit of prophecy within them.

Notice what Revelation 1:9 says, **"I, John, your brother and companion in the suffering and kingdom and patient** endurance that are ours in Jesus, was on the island of Patmos because of the word of God and the testimony of Jesus."

Look at Drawing 7.1 to see what the Spirit of prophecy looks like. The testimony (words) of Jesus IS the Spirit of prophecy. The Holy Spirit hears the testimony of Jesus and delivers it to the servants.

Paul makes it clear in 1 Corinthians that of all the gifts God has given to His people (the church), the greatest is the gift of prophecy. Of all the *graces* given to the church, charity is the greatest. But of the *gifts,* prophecy is the greatest because those who prophesy *edify* (lift up or explain or instruct) the church in the way of God.

The Spirit of prophecy is the mechanism God uses to reach those who are listening. This circular mechanism will be manifest in the last days with great power and authority because God is going to pour out His Spirit in a remarkable way. Follow the pattern in Drawing 7.1.

When the Spirit (HS) speaks to one of the 144,000, and that servant then speaks to an individual (Sam), who is living by faith and following the Spirit in his life, the Spirit within him will confirm what is being said is true, and the circuit is then completed.

Joel 2 says that God is going to pour out His Spirit on all flesh—all 8 billion of us. But first, He's going to pour out His Spirit on His servants. And when the servants speak, if one's heart and mind are open to the leading of the Spirit, he will recognize truth. It will be confirmed as they study the Word.

Revelation 14:12 talks about the suffering the saints are going to endure. It says, **"This calls for patient endurance on the part of the people of God who keep his commands and remain faithful to Jesus."** The suffering will be off the scale.

Look at Revelation 12:17. This verse is speaking of the dragon who is preparing to make war against the woman. **"Then the dragon was enraged at the woman and went off to wage** war against the rest of her offspring—those who keep God's commands and hold fast their testimony about Jesus."

This verse identifies those who obey God's commandments. God knows a lot of people would attempt to get to heaven through works if they could. It's called legalism.

*Legalism*

Legalism is very compatible with our human nature. We learn a certain form of legalism in school. The teacher gives you a test, you want a perfect score. And this perfection is to be attained by any means, even cheating if necessary.

We start learning that by doing perfectly we have done all that can be done. And many people, spiritually, adopt this type of thinking—"If I do what the law commands, I'm perfect."

Now, here's the bad news.

God has designed the end-time test in such a way, we can't possibly pass it unless we can live by faith. It is set up in such a way that we will fail unless we learn how to walk by faith now! If we enter this time period not knowing how to live by faith, the pressure will overcome us and we will justify disobedience and rebellion toward God. That's what sin is.

The three Hebrews: Shadrach, Meshach, and Abednego, could have said on the plain of Dura, "Friends, when the music sounds, let's just kneel here and have a word of prayer for the king." Think of the problems *that* would have solved. The fiery furnace would not have been a threat. They could have rationalized themselves into disobedience. But God clearly states in the second commandment, "Thou shalt not bow down to any graven image."

The test for them was the worship of this graven image. They could have justified their rebellion; they could have justified their sin; they could have explained away the whole story; but, they were prepared for death the morning they went out to that plain. They knew what the test involved and they were prepared to die if necessary. They even told the king, in no uncertain terms, that they would not capitulate to any decree that defied what their God had instructed them to do.

Notice their words to the king, "**If we are thrown into the blazing furnace, the God we serve is able to deliver us from it, and he will deliver us from Your Majesty's hand. But even if he does not, we want you to know, Your Majesty, that we will not serve your gods or worship the image of gold you have set up.**"[1]

You don't 'smart off' like that to somebody who has control over your life, unless you are prepared to lose it. But these men could stand erect before this monarch of the world because they had already bowed before the King of the universe.

God has designed this end-time test in such a way that we cannot possibly survive unless we are willing to live by faith. This test is going to separate the sheep from the goats. It's what the scenario is all about.

You can easily see how the living will judge themselves, and the faith of God's people will be revealed. Notice what Revelation 13:7 says, "**It [the beast] was given power to wage war against God's holy people and to conquer them.**"

The saints are going to be beaten to a pulp. That's what the word *conquer* means.

"**And it was given authority over every tribe, people, language and nation.**" Let me explain what is happening.

Revelation 12:17 says, "**Then the dragon was enraged at the woman and went off to wage war against the rest of her offspring—those who keep God's commands and hold fast their testimony about Jesus.**" This verse states the dragon is preparing to make war upon the remnant.

The remnant live during the Great Tribulation, not at any other time in world history. The remnant does not yet exist. The remnant doesn't exist until we reach the time of wrath during the Great Tribulation.

---

[1] Daniel 3:17–18

Gabriel told Daniel, "I am going to tell you what will happen later in the time of wrath, because the vision concerns the appointed time of the end."[1] He came to Daniel and told him what would happen *later* because the vision concerns an appointed time *at the end of time.*

Based on what this verse says, do you think God has set a date when the end shall come? Yes. The Bible calls it an appointed time. If you have an appointment to see the dentist, there's a specific time to be there. The dentist usually isn't ready to see you when you arrive, but that's beside the point.

Go to Revelation 9:15 and notice what it says about the sixth trumpet. "And the four angels who had been kept ready for this very hour and day and month and year were released to kill a third of mankind." Would you call this an appointment? Yes, the specificity is undeniable. You cannot make an appointment without those four requisites being known.

These four angels have been kept ready for what, in the Greek language, is a punctiliar moment in time, down to the very hour. It won't come early, it won't come late. It will only come right on time.

Notice what Exodus 12:41 says about the Lord's timing, "At the end of the 430 years, to the very day, all the Lord's divisions left Egypt." To the very day, God delivered the children of Israel when He said He would. I can show you that Jesus died on Calvary as the Lamb of God at the precise moment the Passover lamb was to be slain in the temple. God's timing knows no haste, it knows no delay. It is always perfect.

*Time of Wrath*

For the remainder of this chapter, I want to share some of the details concerning what happens during the appointed time of wrath. God has appointed a time for the end to come, and the Bible predicts that the devil is going to physically appear masquerading as God almighty. He will come in clouds

---

[1] Daniel 8:19

of glory with his angels and appear at various times around the world.

John, in Revelation 9, describes this great foe coming down out of the sky. The devil will come down and walk upon the earth. His deception will be so clever that, if possible, it could deceive the very elect.

Those who read their Bibles know that when Jesus comes, He never touches the ground. The saints are resurrected and meet Him in the air.

Paul says in 1 Thessalonians 4:17, **"After that, we who are still alive and are left will be caught up together with them in the clouds to meet the Lord in the air. And so we will be with the Lord forever."** But when the devil comes, he comes claiming to be God.

Notice what Scripture says in Daniel 11:36, **"The king will do as he pleases. He will exalt and magnify himself above every god and will say unheard-of things against the God of gods. He will be successful until the time of wrath is completed, for what has been determined must take place."** Did you notice the words, "every god"?

There are a lot of different gods in this world: the god of the Hindu, the god of the Jew, the god of the Catholic, the god of the Protestant. The part of the verse to especially notice is, **"He will be successful until the time of wrath is completed, for what has been determined must take place."** God has predetermined the Antichrist will be successful for a time. The Bible even says, "It must take place." God has laid this out. This is a plan. The sixth trumpet will blow at the appointed hour, and it will happen on time. That's what the Bible says (in plain Greek).

Look at Revelation 15:1, **"I saw in heaven another great and marvelous sign: seven angels with the seven last plagues— last, because with them God's wrath is completed."**

Now look at Drawing 7.2. Notice there are 7 trumpets and

7 bowls. And with these bowls, the Bible says, God's wrath is completed. The word LAST suggests there are FIRST plaques, which start the wrath of God. There are 7 first plaques (trumpets) and 7 last plagues (bowls).

The neat thing about this is that God, even in His anger, leaves the door of mercy open for a time. When God looks down upon this world He sees the abuse, the sin, the suffering, and the heartache that goes on. He sees it all. And I imagine His patience is wearing thin.

There's a prophetic mechanism that says prophetic things are only understood on or about the time of fulfillment. And, because we are in the time period just before the Great Tribulation begins, the time has come to understand what God is about to do.

For centuries, there has been much talk about Revelation meaning this and that; yet, look at what Daniel 12:4 says, **"But you, Daniel, roll up and seal the words of the scroll until**

**the time of the end."** The phrase *time of the end* implies only the final generation will understand correctly what the book contains.

God sealed up the book of Daniel because only the people who live at the end need to understand what it means. We only need the map if we're traveling the road. I don't know when the Great Tribulation will begin, but I believe it is even at the door.

This is why in Matthew 24 and 25, Jesus, talking to His disciples says, **"Therefore keep watch, because you do not know on what day your Lord will come... because you do not know the day or the hour"**[1]

In the sad story of the ten virgins, when they finally awakened, it was too late for five of them. Well, just as what happened in that story, a great awakening is going to take place before the Lord returns. And it will be the work of God. It will be the outpouring of the Holy Spirit on the 144,000. That is the next prophetic event. It's what we're waiting for. And when we see that happen, we'll know the end is here.

Now, the challenge will be, when we see the outpouring of the Holy Spirit and know the hour has come, will we put our heads in the sand or unite our energies and efforts to help God's servants?

How will we recognize the outpouring of the Holy Spirit? The first evidence will be similar to when John the Baptist was preaching by the Jordan.

People would go and listen to him and say, "There's something different about this man. There's something special and powerful about what he's saying. This is not human wisdom being propagated; he's not just a gifted orator. This man is a prophet who speaks with a penetration that hits home. This is a man of God."

The second evidence will be manifestations of miracles just as it was in the days of the apostles. Peter and John healed the

---

[1] Matthew 24:42; Matthew 25:13

cripple; Paul healed many. There were all kinds of manifestations of power resting on the disciples, and that power confirmed what they said was worth listening to and needed due
consideration. Satan will have his miracle-working messengers
as well. The contest is going to be fierce, but God's Spirit is
greater than all the devil's forces combined.

*Preparing to Harvest*

I want to introduce you to three concepts. The first concept
is, God is going to melt down every religion. There are seven
religious systems throughout the world, and God is going to
show that they are all false.

An example of how this works can be seen in the Worldwide
Church of God. At one time, that church was a large and happy
and prosperous church. But when its leaders concluded there
were things the church was doing wrong and altered them,
80 percent of its membership vanished. The church literally
dissolved overnight.

If some force had attacked that church from outside, its
members would have circled the wagons and stood firm in
their loyalty to defend the church. But when God imploded
the church from within, it simply collapsed and its members
were left in a great lurch. Now they don't know what to believe.

I remember speaking with a friend who had been a member
for more than forty years, and he said, "I've never seen anything like it. I never thought such a thing was possible." I said
to him, "God is going to do this to every church; He just loved
yours most!"

Because when people have their religious loyalties snatched
away, suddenly, they have to rethink their religious paradigms.

And I told my friend, "God loved you so much that He destroyed the loyalty to your church so that you could consider
'what truth is.'"

If you were to go to a Muslim or Jew or Protestant or Catholic, you couldn't tell them anything; they already know what

they want to believe. This is why 95 percent of church goers never change churches. Whatever denomination you're born into, that's the one you die out of. Less than 5 percent of the world's population change churches.

People who haven't been through this type of paradigm shift can't understand it until something compelling knocks them off their feet. God is going to melt down all churches so that He can see who is faithful.

Revelation does not speak of a true church. Revelation speaks of a body of people who love truth! God's people come from every nation, kindred, and tongue, and they are in many different churches. And when He melts down their churches, the only thing that will be left standing is His people!

When I was little boy, there was a pantomime exercise we used to do in church. All the kids would put their hands together with their fingers interlocking and say, "Here's the church and here's the steeple, open the door and see all the people." I've often thought about that demonstration because when God looks into His church, I wonder if all of them are really His people.

The second concept is found in Revelation 6:9. It says, **"When he [Jesus] opened the fifth seal, I saw under the altar the souls of those who had been slain because of the word of God and the testimony they had maintained."** There are going to be many martyrs for the cause of Christ during this time period. Millions will die for their faith.

Look at Drawing 7.2. In the Old Testament, the sanctuary had a courtyard and a little building that held the Holy and Most Holy places. At the entrance to the courtyard sat the altar of burnt offering (ABO), and underneath this altar was a little bucket (BUC) used for excess blood when sacrifices were brought and offered. When this bucket was full of blood, it was taken outside the camp, its contents set afire and destroyed. The significance of this is that the *blood of sacrifices* went into this bucket.

The imagery used in heaven's Temple is the same. The Sanctuary on earth is a parallel of what is in heaven. This visual is describing blood from "the souls of those who had been slain." What John is telling us is, these are sacrifices (martyrs) God is allowing to save others. What is more convincing to the testimony and power of truth than a martyr who intelligently and calmly—without rancor or anger—stands firmly for his faith and goes to his death? John Foxe wrote in his *Book of Martyrs*, "The blood of martyrs is fertilizer to the gospel."

Many are going to die for their faith because of A) the Word of God, and B) the testimony of Jesus which they hold and will not let go. People who are innocent will die; they will go to their death holding on to the promise of God. But, understand, every martyr is victorious. You cannot be more victorious than to go to your death for the cause of Christ.

In Revelation 6:10–11, these martyrs called out in a loud voice, **"They called out in a loud voice, 'How long, Sovereign Lord, holy and true, until you judge the inhabitants of the earth and avenge our blood?' Then each of them was given a white robe, and they were told to wait a little longer, until the full number of their fellow servants, their brothers and sisters, were killed just as they had been."**

Throughout Revelation, John keeps a clear distinction between the people and the prophets. Many of the 144,000—if not all of them—will die in the line of duty. They are the ones who are told to wait. God has already decided how many sacrifices He will allow. It will be a large number for two reasons.

First, those who are weary of the struggle are put to sleep so as to miss most of the tribulation. Second, and more importantly, the most extreme thing God can do to impress a human heart is martyrdom. Let me explain.

Suppose God allows 100 million martyrs to die, and as a result of these sacrifices, 50 people decide to give their lives to Christ just before the end. These 50 people will feel indebted throughout eternity! They will say, "God was willing to give a hundred million people to impress me with the importance of surrendering my life. I'm that important to God that He would do that? What a God!"

Now, if you can understand this, you can begin to understand what God gave when He gave Jesus. Jesus is worth more than a hundred million people. He's worth more than the whole world! And once we consider what God has given for our salvation, we should be so overcome with God's goodness and love that we cannot refuse His offer.

This is why He's going to melt down the churches, so people can consider truth for what it is. He's designed the test so that we can only pass it, and remain faithful, if we are willing to live by faith. Every means of self-support will be cut off. All of those who receive the mark of the beast, do so, because they can't trust God.

But wait… I want to give you some hope.

Look at Revelation 13:10. God says, **"If anyone is to go into captivity, into captivity they will go. If anyone is to be killed with the sword, with the sword they will be killed."**

This means God knows what the plan is for your life during this time period. And if He has decided that you are to go into captivity, you're going; don't worry about it. Just do everything you can before you get there. If you're going to jail for your faith, just make sure you go kicking and screaming; but, do all of that before they come to get you. God has a plan to save man because He is anxious to save us all. If God has already determined that you're going to be a martyr, don't worry. He's in charge.

Notice this sentence, **"This calls for patient endurance and faithfulness on the part of God's people."** Patience and endurance are two of the toughest words in the English language.

When you walk by faith, you don't always understand where you're going. You can't always see the end. You're out on a limb, but you have peace within. I am fully convinced of the things

I'm sharing. I know the story can be frightening. Dwelling on devastation is frightening. But it doesn't have to be, once we understand that it's part of God's plan to save us.

I hear people saying all the time, "Larry, I'm scared of those beasts in Revelation. I'm scared of what God is about to do. It frightens me. I don't want to know the details." I'm sure in Noah's day, the antediluvians didn't want to consider a flood. But it looks to me like, in Noah's day, they should have considered the ark. Why focus on the flood? Focus on the ark. In the same way, why focus on what happens to the saints during the time of trouble? Rather, focus on the victory of the saints. We're going home! Our troubles are going to be over!

In Hebrews 12:2, the Bible says that Christ, **"For the joy set before him he endured the cross, scorning its shame, and sat down at the right hand of the throne of God."** There won't be any sickness—no surgeries, no scars, no aging, no heartache, no suffering, no tears—it'll be over. We're going home! And that thrills my heart!

God has designed this whole setup in such a way as to rescue and save the maximum number of people. When God calls you to live by faith, with that calling comes an enabling. You do not have to approach this in human strength. If you do, you will fail. But, if you will take hold of the hand of the Master, you can walk on water! You can do the impossible, for through faith all things are possible. *That's what this story is all about!*

The third concept I want you to consider is that Jesus went to Calvary realizing that He might never come back; that decision was the Father's call, not His. When Jesus went to the cross, He suffered the wrath of God (second death) for you and me. And as He hung there and called out, **"My God, my God, why have you forsaken me?"**[1] He DIED without knowing He would ever come back! That is what the second death is—dying and never coming back.

Jesus, a member of the Godhead, and Creator of the

---

[1] Matthew 27:46

universe, was willing to cease to exist so that one sinner could have eternal life. What a Savior! What a God! If He's willing to do that then His words, "**Surely I am with you always, to the very end of the age**" can be taken at face value.[1]

Whether our end is sooner or later doesn't matter. Either way we'll get to see His face. Whatever God has in mind for me is okay, because I know that with Him we are more than conquerors; we have overcome the world through faith. Faith will take you places you never thought possible—ultimately to heaven.

Pray with me.

Father in heaven, it's so wonderful to read and to study and to search out the riches of the gospel, and to see the wonderful plan you have for your children. Oh God, help us to appropriate these truths in our lives. Give us a willing heart. Give us a sweet spirit. Give us and enable us with all the graces that the Spirit brings.

Thank you for the promise of transforming us. We can see the manifestation of your power, even now, and we know it is but a sample of what we will become. Thank you for the privilege of studying your Word. Continue your blessings on us this day is our prayer, in Jesus' wonderful name, amen.

> I pray you've been touched in reading this, and that Jesus has brought you the joy and happiness that I know. May God bless you and be with you.

---

[1] Matthew 28:20

*If you will take hold of the hand of the Master, you can walk on water! You can do the impossible.*

*That's what this story is all about!*